D0776244

Rosema

A Sober Mom's Guide to Recovery

Rosemary O'Connor is such a warm and experienced companion for women trying to manage the difficult and exhilarating
path of sober motherhood. She has such a good sense of humor,
and a lot of both practical and spiritual wisdom. I wish I'd had
this book when I had my child in early recovery—I would have
gone less crazy, less often, and had amazing tools with which to
navigate and enjoy both passionate challenges a lot more.

—ANNE LAMOTT, author of *Traveling Mercies,*
Small Victories, Operating Instructions,
and *Help, Thanks, Wow*

I have had the opportunity to work with Rosemary O'Connor
and her excellent Recovery Services for several years. She is a
role model for Twelve Step recovery. Her services for women
and outstanding continuum of care have contributed a great
deal by fulfilling the need in the San Francisco Bay Area for
excellent treatment of addiction.

—DR. DAVID E. SMITH, diplomate,
American Board of Addiction Medicine,
and founder, Haight Ashbury Free Clinic

A Sober Mom's Guide to Recovery

TAKING CARE OF YOURSELF
TO TAKE CARE OF YOUR KIDS

ROSEMARY O'CONNOR

Hazelden Publishing
Center City, Minnesota 55012
hazelden.org/bookstore

Library of Congress Cataloging-in-Publication Data

O'Connor, Rosemary.
    A sober mom's guide to recovery : taking care of yourself to take care of your kids / Rosemary O'Connor.
      pages cm
Summary: "For mothers in recovery from substance use disorders, Rosemary O'Connor offers her own hard-won wisdom, helping women navigate the challenges of sober self-care and care of children"— Provided by publisher.
ISBN 978-1-61649-602-9 (paperback) — ISBN 978-1-61649-624-1 (ebook)
1. Recovering alcoholics—Family relationships. 2. Women alcoholics
Rehabilitation. 3. Women alcoholics—Family relations. 4. Mothers—Alcohol use. 5. Children of alcoholics. 6. Parent and child. I. Title.
    HV5132.O36 2015
    362.292'40852—dc23
                                                                            2015020053

Editor's note
The names, details, and circumstances may have been changed to protect the privacy of those mentioned in this publication.
    This publication is not intended as a substitute for the advice of health care professionals.
    Alcoholics Anonymous, AA, and the Big Book are registered trademarks of Alcoholics Anonymous World Services, Inc.

19 18 17 16 15   1 2 3 4 5 6

Cover design: Theresa Jaeger Gedig
Interior design: Terri Kinne
Developmental editor: Sid Farrar
Production editor: Mindy Keskinen
Typesetting: Bookmobile Design & Digital Publisher Services

This book is dedicated to my three amazing children. You all have been my greatest teachers. At one time you were the only reasons I wanted to live, and you saved my life. I decided to get sober because I loved each of you so much, and then I learned to love myself and stay sober for me. Being a sober mother to each of you is God's greatest gift to me.

This book is also dedicated to my mother and father who provided me guidance, unconditional love, and a strong foundation for my faith in God. There are no words that adequately express my gratitude for all the blessings I have received from both of you.

Contents

Acknowledgments

I could not have written this book without the help, love, and support of so many people. Lori Odisio, for saving my life. Lori Jean Glass, for helping me become the loving, sober mother my children deserve. Kate Webster, for supporting me through some of my darkest days of depression with her magical English cups of tea. Michele Bonsignore, for unconditional love and acceptance. Beth Holland, who has added so much laughter and fun to my sobriety. My sister, Colleen O'Connor, who was always there to help with my children during the most difficult times in my life. For my sponsors and all the women who reached their hand out to me and showed me the way. Thank you all for showing me the light when my world was so dark, for loving me, and teaching me how to love and forgive myself. Thank you all for helping me grow into the woman God intended me to be.

My deepest gratitude to the most amazing writing coach and friend, Diane Conway. Thank you for sharing this journey with me. This book would not have been possible without you. I also thank Sid Farrar, senior editor at Hazelden Publishing, for his guidance and enthusiasm. He added one more reason for me to be grateful on the publication of my first book.

• • •

Preface

I was an out-of-control alcoholic mother and after years of trying to control my drinking, I hit my bottom in 1999 after drinking all night and not coming home to my three small children. Throughout my journey in recovery I looked for books that could help me with certain challenges that I faced raising my kids and found nothing specific to mothers in recovery. *A Sober Mom's Guide to Recovery* is my way of giving what I so desperately needed to other mothers who face the everyday challenges of being a sober mom. My intention is to share real-life challenges sober mothers can identify with, and the practical tools that helped me transform my life and stay sober. My hope is to support mothers who are trying to stay sober no matter what challenges they may face. In doing so they are giving themselves and their children a priceless gift, which not even the most profound words could begin to explain.

I began my journey in recovery in 1999 and understand the challenges of staying sober and rebuilding a life. Over the past ten years as an experienced life coach, I have taught hundreds of people how to bring about positive changes in their personal and professional lives. I founded ROC Recovery Services, whose mission is to help women recover from the devastating effects of addiction and to teach them how to live a rewarding life of purpose and meaningful connection to themselves and others.

• • •

1

Hitting Bottom

Recovery is not so bad. It's kinda like walking backward through molasses up to your crotch with your legs tied together.

— ANNE WILSON SCHAEF

I promised myself I was only going out for two drinks. I told the eleven-year-old babysitter I'd be home in a couple of hours—no later than nine. I walked out the door on my way to a fancy charity event, the Fireman's Ball at the San Francisco Yacht Club. I was all dressed up in a long, sequined gown, high heels, hair and makeup to the nines (for me it was all about looking good on the outside). At the event, with drink in hand, I started chatting up a guy. I was doing straight shots of tequila and quickly spent $200 buying drinks from the bar—what every classy lady does. Mr. Not-So-Prince-Charming invited me to continue the party at his place. I remember following in my car, gripping the steering wheel, trying to steer in a straight line. The next thing I remember is waking up in Mr. Not-So-Prince-Charming's bed at ten the next morning, thirteen hours after I'd told the babysitter I'd be back.

I drove home overcome with dread, silently promising never to drink again. The scene that met me there was Dickensian: my three children were lined up on the sofa in their pajamas, eyes wide with horror, staring at me. On either side of them were my best friend, Lori, whose daughter had been babysitting, and my estranged husband. They didn't look too friendly, either. And no wonder—I was still wearing the sequined gown from the night before, which I'd thrown up on, and my hair and makeup were in shambles.

Lori looked me straight in the eye. "You'd better get hold of yourself," she said, and stormed out. My husband looked at me with utter disgust. I got the message in his glare: *If you don't get your act together, I'll take these kids away.*

As he gathered the kids to go upstairs for their stuff, my five-year-old son asked me, "Mommy, are you okay?"

I was not. For the first time in the twenty-one years I'd been drinking, I acknowledged there was something really wrong with me. I said, "No, Mommy is not okay." He grabbed me and hugged me. Then he ran upstairs crying.

My soon-to-be ex-husband left with my children and went to his house. I was alone, an empty shell, physically, spiritually, and emotionally bankrupt. What I feared most was that I would continue to do the same thing over and over and lose my children. This was not the mother I intended to be. That was my bottom. And I knew in that moment that if I didn't get help, five o'clock would roll around and I'd be drunk once again.

Since then, I have worked with countless women and I know this scene has played itself out both in multimillion-dollar homes and in tenements. Our social standing, education, and self-knowledge don't matter. When the alcohol or drugs get hold of us, we are taken over. We do things when we're drinking and using that make us weep bitter tears when the high wears off.

We are basically good women and mothers, and under normal circumstances we would take good care of ourselves and fiercely protect our children. We can't imagine how we let this happen, how we could lose control. We feel disgust, shame, and hopelessness. We vow never to let this happen again.

I had made that promise more times than I could remember. But now, for the first time, I listened to a voice in my head. *Ask for help,* it said. I went to the phone book, found the number for Alcoholics Anonymous, and called. The woman who answered the phone asked me to join her at an AA meeting. There I found women who used to feel the same way I did. At last I knew I was not alone. I stopped drinking one day at a time as other women taught me how to face life without a drink or a drug. In my recovery—fifteen years as of this writing—I have found peace, compassion, and forgiveness for myself. I respect myself and love the woman I am today. (Most of the time!) Best of all, I am present for my children, and they love me.

Getting clean and sober is like dropping a single rock into a still pond and sending healing ripples out to our family, friends, and all the people who share our journey of recovery.

Sober Mom's Tools
for Climbing Up after Hitting Bottom

1. Take the first step: in the recovery process, the first step is admitting that we have a problem. For me, the evidence that my life was unmanageable was right in front of me that morning I came home to face my children. Using my story as an example, write about your own "hitting bottom" experience. If you're new to recovery, it might be painful to put it in writing, but it can help you take that first step to admitting you have a problem. Even after facing my children that morning, I still had my doubts as to whether I was a full-blown alcoholic. But it was suggested that I write down my last ten drinking episodes. In doing this it became quite evident that my drinking was nowhere near normal. It was clear that

when I started with a glass of wine I never knew where I'd end up or what I'd do.

2. Ask for help: this is the single most important action we can take to liberate us from isolation and loneliness. For me, and for many other women, it's easier and more helpful to reach out to another woman. We are not meant to do life alone. If you are still trying to deal with a drinking or using problem alone, pick up the phone and call for help. You can get immediate help by calling Alcoholics Anonymous, or if your drug of choice isn't alcohol, you may want to try Narcotics Anonymous; both groups are free and available twenty-four hours a day. You don't have to do this by yourself. (See the Recommended Resources at the back of this book for these and other Twelve Step programs.)

3. If you're reluctant to get help for yourself, do it for the sake of your children. Addiction is a progressive, fatal disease. It's not a matter of *if* this disease will get worse, it's a matter of *when.* Many mothers have lost custody of their children due to their addiction.

4. If you are still questioning "if" you have a problem with your drinking or using, go to www.aa.org, read the pamphlet *A.A. for the Woman* and take the fifteen-question test.

• • •

2

Guilt

Guilt: The gift that keeps on giving.
— ERMA BOMBECK

Guilt is the constant companion of the alcoholic or addict, maybe even more so for a woman. Every mother feels guilt about her parenting from time to time. That's doubly true for women who have created drama and caused distress for their children by drinking or using—possibly inflicting psychological damage. Here's one story from my past that still makes me cringe. Due to my drinking, I was separated from my husband, but was still living in my beautiful Northern California home with my three children, ages two, five, and eight. I was the top sales person in my company and still getting promoted. I had the perfect job for a drunk, taking clients to lunch and dinner, with lots of drinks on the company dime. Things looked good on the outside but they were rotten within.

My girlfriends were taking me out to celebrate my thirty-sixth birthday. As I sipped my fine wine in a beautiful crystal glass, I got dressed in a hot black miniskirt, high heels, and a low-cut top, cleavage and all. I kissed my kids goodbye and went off to a local chic restaurant where I drank my dinner with my girlfriends.

Then we adjourned one block down to the local dive bar to continue the party and seek the attention of colorful low-life companions. The bouncer at the door thought things were looking up as five glamorous gals appeared, and the usual gnarly crowd all looked up from their drinks as we graced them with our presence. That same bouncer escorted us out the door forty-five minutes later for picking fights with the so-called gnarly crowd. The classy girls quickly went from class to trash.

The party continued at my house, where my kids were fast asleep and I dismissed the babysitter. We called some guys, grabbed some liquor, shed our clothes, and headed for the hot tub in the backyard. Things quickly spiraled down, and once again I became a woman who disgusted me the morning after.

I heard my two-year-old son wake up crying, so I headed upstairs toward the bedrooms, still dripping wet, and picked up my crying child. And then, boom, I caught a glimpse of myself in the mirror with babe in arms and was shocked to see that Mr. Hot Tub had followed me and was behind me trying to kiss me.

As if that wasn't bad enough, I realized the sun was coming up and I needed to take my five-year-old son for his entrance interview at our local Catholic school. I had an hour to sober up, get my child ready, and drive to the school. Later, as my son held my hand and we approached the nun who would do the interview, I felt the soul-wrenching shame only an addicted mother can feel.

Before recovery this was the picture of what I had become—a drunk, scared, and horrible mom. A mom who knew only one way to deal with these feelings: to drink again.

That's one of many of my "cringe stories," and if you're like me, you probably have some of your own. After we get sober and begin swapping stories with other recovering women, for the first time we will feel as if we aren't carrying the burden alone because other women have done the same things we have. Hearing another woman's story and identifying with her was the first time I felt any relief from guilt.

I thought the feeling of guilt would end once I stopped drinking. But from time to time friends or family brought up an incident from our past, and out of nowhere the shame and guilt would rise up in me automatically. The first time this happened and I was able to face my guilt without drinking, I was ninety days sober, at my sponsor's seven-year sobriety party. The people at the party were sitting in a circle, taking turns naming the ways in which my sponsor had changed as a result of her sobriety. Suddenly my nine-year-old daughter announces, "Yeah, and my mom doesn't yell at me anymore!"

Everyone laughed, but I was horrified, overwhelmed by guilt and fear that I'd irreparably damaged my kids for life. That night I sat my kids down and made them a promise. If I yelled at them, I said, I'd give them a quarter. My five-year-old son looked at his sister and said, "We're going to be rich!" They were excited about the money, but I needed to deal with feelings about what a horrible mother I had been. Thank God for the Seventh Step of the Alcoholics Anonymous program, in which we ask for the defects we uncovered in our Fourth Step to be removed. And thank God for the promises that follow the Ninth Step: "We will not regret the past nor wish to shut the door on it," as the "Big Book" of *Alcoholics Anonymous* says in chapter 6. (The Twelve Steps of AA are found at the back of this book.) If we continue to beat ourselves up about our past and wallow in self-pity, we will not be present for our children, and, worst of all, we pass down our shame to our children.

Another time early in my sobriety when I was suffering from remorse about how my drinking and alcoholic behavior had damaged my children beyond repair, I was given a moment of grace. I was walking to the beach with my father and my adorable three-year-old son. My father asked my son what he wanted to be when he grew up. Without missing a beat my son said, "I want to be an alcoholic." I was still feeling so shameful and worried about what my father was thinking about my alcoholism. *Oh good God!* I thought. Yet even though I was afraid of what else my son might say if the conversation continued, I decided to ask him why. He responded, "Because alcoholics don't yell, and they laugh a lot." Joseph didn't understand what an alcoholic really was. But what he did know was that when I drank, I screamed and yelled a lot, and when I stopped drinking I stopped yelling. What my son didn't know was that I was able to stop yelling with a lot of help from my sponsor and through working the Twelve Steps of AA.

As we continued to walk toward the beach, I flashed back to a few months before I got sober when my father had looked at me and said, "You have got to stop yelling at your kids." Now, as I felt my toes in the sand and savored the precious time spent with my father and son, I was overwhelmed with the feeling of grace. It was at that moment that I realized the miracle of the Twelve Steps and how they were healing my family and me in more ways I ever could have imagined. I didn't have to beat myself up about the past anymore. I could forgive myself. I was making my living amends by being present with my family and not screaming at my children. And I realized that staying sober is the best gift you can give your children and the legacy of your family.

Sober Mom's Tools for Overcoming Guilt

1. Make a list of all the things you do well as a mom. Be kind to yourself. As Rosanne Barr said, "If the kids are still alive at five p.m. and the house hasn't burned down, I've done a good

job." Ask the supportive people in your life why they think you're a good mom. You might be surprised how many good qualities your own children will be able to list.

2. Stop beating yourself up! Most women have a PhD in negative self-talk. Our Inner Critic yammers at us all day every day. Mine is very creative in finding ways to beat me up: *I'm not enough, and never will be. Every other mother is* _____. (Pick one: kinder, more accomplished, more loving, you name it.) Here's an exercise I do with my clients: I bring them to a mirror, have them look themselves in the eye and say the following: "I love you. I like you. I forgive you." Just about every time, they break down in tears as they—at least in that moment—find release from their guilt. Try writing the phrases above on your bathroom mirror. If you find yourself guilt-tripping or "shoulding" all over yourself (*I should have done this, I shouldn't have done that*), repeat the phrases as a mantra to chase those negative thoughts away: "I love you. I like you. I forgive you."

3. Prayer to remove guilt: "Dear Higher Power, please remove my feelings of guilt, let me see myself as you do: perfect, whole, and complete."

4. If you find it difficult to quiet your Inner Critic, Google the phrase "Bob Newhart Stop It," click on the YouTube video, watch it, and take Bob's advice.

• • •

3

Exhaustion

*In the event of loss of cabin pressure the oxygen mask
over your head will drop down. If you are sitting next to
a small child, or someone who is acting like a small child,
please do us all a favor and put on your mask first.
If you are traveling with two or more children, please take
a moment to decide which one is your favorite.
Help that one first, then work your way down.*

— FLIGHT ATTENDANT ANNOUNCEMENT

Have you ever reached the point of complete exhaustion? Of course you have—you're a woman. And as a mother you are an expert in the exhaustion department. Add to that being a mother trying to recover from addiction, and exhaustion becomes a way of life. If you're like me, a lot of this comes from our tendency to overdo everything to prove to ourselves (and everybody else) that we're okay, that we're competent, and that we aren't going to screw things up the way we did when we were drinking and using.

One day when I was newly sober and working full time, going through a divorce, and raising three kids, I was complaining to my therapist about how tired I was. He suggested I take a twenty-minute nap in the afternoon, between work and picking up the kids. I truly thought this man was from Mars: he might as well suggest I fly to the moon. The concept of a nap was to-tally foreign to me. My mother used to take naps when we were kids, and I thought she was crazy. Well, she had seven kids, so I'm sure naps saved her. Today two of my kids are grown and out of the house and I still find myself exhausted. I can't blame my exhaustion on a husband, boyfriend, or kids. The common denominator is me. I need to slow down, build in some quiet time, and learn how to say no to some of the requests people make of me. I need to follow my therapist's advice, and my mom's example, and start taking naps!

When I was about five years sober and still running around like a chicken with its head cut off, I had been feeling ill for quite some time but never went to the doctor. I kept putting it off because I told myself I didn't have time. Finally I was in so much pain I went to the doctor and found out I had a terrible infection. She sent me home with a prescription, but on my way I told myself I was too busy to get it filled. I had promised my boys I'd take them to the Giants game that night. I told myself I'd get it filled tomorrow; tonight I'd just grin and bear the pain.

The boys were very happy and enjoyed the baseball game, but I shivered through the cold night until we finally got home at about eleven thirty. At five in the morning I woke up with my entire body shaking uncontrollably. Scared, I had no idea what was happening. I yelled for my daughter who was so scared that she called both 911 and my best friend who lived up the street. In no time at all I looked up to three handsome firemen and two paramedics surrounding me in my tiny little bedroom. Boy, I wished I'd worn cuter pajamas, but at least I'd gone to bed with my makeup on, I thought. The next thing I knew I was whisked away on a stretcher as my children's eyes filled with fear. Thank God my friend Lori had shown up and was there to get the kids ready for school.

At the hospital the nurses hooked me up to several beeping machines, and when the doctor showed up he asked me all sorts of questions. After he was done, I asked him how long all of this would take, explaining that I had to get home because I had a lot of things to do. The doctor looked at me quite sternly and said, "Ma'am, your kidneys are shutting down. I'm going to have to admit you to the hospital for a few days if you don't promise me that you'll lie down and rest for a few days at home. If you'll do that, I will let you go home in a few hours." I wasn't sure if being called "ma'am" was worse than my kidneys shutting down, but I was able to register how serious the doctor sounded. I thought of the look on my kids' faces when I was whisked out the door and put in the ambulance, and I promised the doctor (and myself) that I'd go home and rest. I made a pledge then to start taking better care of myself and to put my needs right up there with the children's needs. I realized how important it was to take care of myself so I could take care of my kids. At that moment it hit me how much danger I'd put myself in by trying to be everything to everybody. I finally understood the analogy of putting the oxygen mask on myself *first* and then putting it on my children next.

As I lay in bed over the next few days I made a list on a sheet of paper. On the left side I listed all the areas where I had been an over-doer. On the right side I listed some ways I would cut back. Here are some examples. Every night I'd been cooking dinner and doing all the dishes. That night I told my kids I would cook dinner and *they* would do the dishes. They didn't like it, but I laughed to myself remembering a quote I had read by Ben Bergor: "It is amazing how quickly the kids learn to drive a car, yet are unable to understand the lawn mower, snowblower, or vacuum cleaner." I was usually the mom who did all the driving to wherever my kids wanted to go. I decided to set up car pools for school, sports, birthday parties, and all the other places they needed to be. If the kids needed shoes, I told them the dollar amount I would pay for shoes. If they wanted the more expensive latest fashion, they could pay the difference. Or I told them I'd buy one shoe and they could either buy the second shoe or hop around on one foot! They never chose the latter.

On one of the many days I was in "mommy overwhelm" mode, I called my sponsor to complain about how my children kept asking me again and again for blah blah blah. I told her I kept telling them no, but then I'd get so tired of saying no that I'd just give in and say yes. She told me to get a large piece of paper, write on it in black ink the words *NO MEANS NO,* and hang it on the refrigerator. I said, "What a great idea for them—I think it will really work." She quickly said, "Oh no, this isn't for them—it's for you." What a concept! Some days it gets so bad I put a *No Means No* sticky note on my forehead.

I have worked as a life coach with many married, newly sober mothers who come to me saying they have no idea why they're miserable in their marriage. When these women first meet with me, most have no idea how exhausted they really are. I tell them that exhaustion can kill intimacy and a marriage. I ask them, when was the last time they went away overnight with their partner or had a date, just the two of them? Most of these mothers come up with the excuses of no money or no time. I point out that they found plenty of time and money to go drink and use. I also ask these women when was the last time they made love to their partner, and most are too embarrassed to tell me because it's been so long. The excuse I hear, and that I'm sure their partner or spouse hears too, is "I'm just too tired." Sometimes I kick these mothers out of my office right then and tell them to go take the money they were paying me and use the hour to take their partner out to lunch.

I also suggest they take their to-do list, cut half the items off it, and use that extra time to rest. If they have children, I tell them to order pizza, put the kids to bed early, and make love to their partner that night. When they look at me with shock, I remind them that they made an appointment with me because they wanted to change, and if they wanted to find someone who will listen to them complain, I am definitely not the right life coach for them!

Sober Mom's Tools
for Overcoming Exhaustion

1. Your to-do list or (*not*-to-do list): Take a sheet of paper and draw a line vertically down the middle to make two columns. On the left side, write: "For Me to Do Today." On the right side write: "God to Do for Me Today." Now, only the most necessary items—those that have to be done today or people will die—go in your "My" column. Everything else has to go in God's column. The things in God's column will be things that need to be done but not necessarily this very day. You can also add things that you wish for in God's column; you won't know how these will manifest themselves, but you've given your Higher Power the job. If you do this exercise every day, it will relieve stress so you are not carrying the world on your shoulders. You will notice that the items in God's column frequently get done in ways you could never have imagined.

2. There are so many things we have no control over. Practice releasing people, situations, and things by repeating, "That's not in my job description!" You will gain freedom and some time for yourself when you quit worrying about everything you can't do in the first place.

3. Give yourself a "Mommy time-out" by taking a bubble bath, doing five minutes of deep breathing and meditation (go to your peaceful place), or doing anything else that restores you. If the kids are home, tell them Mommy needs a time-out and they could help so much by fixing their own lunch, mopping the kitchen floor, and so on.

4. Quick fixes: Beg a friend to take your kids for an hour, then move. (Just kidding about moving, but you can pretend you're in a new city with no responsibilities for an hour.) Surrender the Martha Stewart cape: tear one of her pictures into little tiny pieces. Post on Facebook that you've left the country indefinitely. Serve cereal for dinner.

• • •

4

Loneliness

When we cannot bear to be alone,
it means we do not properly value the only companion
we will have from birth to death—ourselves.

— EDA LESHAN

Loneliness is one of the most difficult human emotions. It can feel like a hole in the bottom of the gut, or a deep, aching longing in the heart, or both. The addict runs from loneliness in many ways: through drugs, alcohol, sex, shopping, bingeing, purging, overeating, gambling, isolating, raging at others, controlling, enmeshment, busyness, overworking, over-volunteering. Oh, and shopping. Did I mention shopping? These quick fixes do the trick at first, but as with all addictive behaviors, the high or distraction quickly wears off and we're back to feeling lonely and isolated. We pick it up "just one more time"—the drug, the alcohol, the lover, the credit card, the carton of ice cream— and then we're left with that deeper hole of self-loathing and demoralization.

There's a difference between being alone and loneliness. You can be alone, by yourself, and not feel lonely. Learning to be alone is a healthy skill to learn in recovery so we find out that we'll live if we don't depend on the usual people, places, and things that have kept us distracted from our feelings. Many women are terrified of being alone. On the other hand, many of us *choose* to isolate because we are terrified at the thought of having to connect to another human being.

Loneliness is the deep spiritual longing to connect with a Higher Power, ourselves, and other human beings—the very things that our addictions had cut us off from at an emotional level. It has nothing to do with the number of people we have around; we can feel just as lonely in a crowded room as when we're at home by ourselves. I know many wives who are terribly lonely even though their husbands come home every night and spend quality time with them. I grew up as one of seven kids born in the span of nine years so there were always a lot of people around me. I was very popular at school and I've always had a lot of friends and can socialize with anyone. I felt comfortable around lots of people and loved big parties and crowds. I went from high school to college dorm where all of us girls hung out together. From college I went to live with girlfriends. I then got married and had my first child one year later. I was always busy, busy, busy.

I remember one particular day after I got divorced and my kids were at my former husband's house: the quiet at home was actually chilling. For the first time I faced the pain of being alone, and it scared me. On more than one occasion, I was actually doubled over in pain from loneliness, despite the many loving people in my life. It felt like there was nothing to live for and no one cared for me. I was sure I would die an old woman alone with cats crawling all over me. I was sure this feeling would never pass and that it might actually kill me.

When I got sober and first felt the feelings of loneliness, I was even more terrified. I had no idea what to do with this feeling—other than drinking. To admit to another person that

I felt lonely was out of the question, because I was busy making others think I had it all together and was doing great.

One day in a Twelve Step meeting, a man shared that he'd rather admit to a serious crime than to say he felt lonely. The room was silent for what seemed like hours. Then one brave soul after another talked about loneliness. Although I didn't know all of the people who were talking, I suddenly felt our souls connect on a deep level I'd never experienced before. A peace came over me and I heard a voice in my head say, *You are not alone.* I now understood the depth of my addiction. It wanted me to feel so lonely that the only solution for me was to drink or use.

At the end of the meeting when the Promises were read from chapter 6 of the Big Book, I heard one of them loud and clear and it penetrated my soul: "We will comprehend the word serenity and we will know peace." I added another promise that I hoped would result from finding peace: "We will begin to enjoy being alone." At first I didn't really believe it would happen, but it has.

I truly believe this is why I kept coming back to meeting after meeting and why I continue to come back to Twelve Step meetings today. For me, it's not just about not drinking; it's about feeling connected to my own spirit so I can feel genuinely connected to others.

Learning to be alone was scary, the last thing I wanted to tackle. But I realized that I couldn't go on running from my tender inner self. It was a matter of trusting myself and honoring my feelings. In her hauntingly beautiful song *Gentle with Myself,* Karen Drucker sings, "I hold myself like a newborn baby child."

My sponsor suggested I do things to honor myself. She had me buy myself flowers, take myself to the movies and dinner alone (oh boy, that was hard!). I cooked a fabulous dinner for myself, as if I was having a hot date over. I pulled out my china, set the table, and lit the candles. Each time I practiced one of these new behaviors I came out on the other side a little bit stronger, with a little more self-confidence in the bank, knowing I could survive the difficult feelings of being alone and not drink or use.

Many clients tell me they have no idea who their "real self" is, or what they like and don't like. When we're not connected to our own spirit and have no idea who we truly are, we try to attach to another person, hoping they'll make us feel whole. It's like walking around with an empty cup with a hole in the bottom, going from person to person saying, *Fill me up.* We look down at the cup and can't understand why we feel so empty.

I needed to learn to be quiet and connect to my Higher Power. I needed to learn to slow down and just *be* with myself. I needed to get to know me.

Getting to know myself was awkward at first—all new healthy behavior is—but I kept stretching myself with my alone times. And it paid off. I was no longer *lonely* when alone as I discovered the tender spirit within, the inner child who'd been waiting for me. My favorite alone times were the drives I'd take up the coast with just the view and me! They became adventures and I actually enjoyed the freedom of pleasing no one but myself. It was liberating. These drives turned into overnights, then weekends. I even went to Spain and spent three days alone, barely speaking to anyone with my very poor Spanglish. Could this be me, Miss Crowd-Loving-Party-Girl? It *was* me, and I discovered there actually *was* someone home inside, and I met her and liked her!

Today I love my own time. I crave it and get really bitchy if I don't take it. Right now I'm planning a trip to Yosemite by myself and there isn't anyone I want to go with more than myself, and that is a frickin' miracle. When I took myself to Hawaii for five days alone, my mother said, "Why don't you ask someone to go with you? Won't you be lonely?" I told her, quite frankly, "The only people I'm inviting are me, myself, and I."

If we don't learn to heal this deep, dark feeling of loneliness, it can have negative effects on our children. To compensate for their loneliness, some mothers become enmeshed with their children, which can suffocate them and harm their emotional growth. This enmeshment can also damage a marriage because all the focus goes on the children, which leaves no room or time for the couple. The clingy wife or girlfriend who is attached to her partner at the hip because she's afraid to be alone can send that person running to their cave and posting guards by the door.

Sober Mom's Tools
for Overcoming Loneliness

1. Breathe! Sit quietly with your eyes closed. Breathe deeply into the part of your body where you feel the ache of loneliness. Keep doing this even if it feels like it's going to kill you. (Rest assured: no one has ever died from sitting and breathing into an aching heart. What *does* kill people is running from this pain by acting out an addiction.)

2. Go deep inside and feel the presence of your Higher Power. Look there for the strength, warmth, safety, and love that you feel is missing in you. Your spirit has a message for you in this place; sit long enough to hear it. You might hear it in words; you might feel it in your body. You will come to know that loneliness is just a text message from your Higher Power saying it wants a date with you.

3. Ask yourself out on a date. We can spend a lot of time and energy trying to find someone who wants to do something with us like going to the movies. Take your Big Girl self by the hand and march up to the box office, buy a ticket for one, choose exactly where you want to sit, and enjoy the movie.

4. Make a list of things you'd like to do. If you don't know what they are (like most of us in early recovery), think of what you liked as a child or wished you could have done as a child. Did you ride a bike, roller skate, dance, hike, put on plays, paint, or play an instrument? Choose one today and do it. You don't have to do it for the rest of your life or become the world's best at it.

5. Pray this prayer: "God, please take away my emptiness and loneliness. Illuminate the dark places within me and guide me with your light. I know that I matter to you and that I am on this Earth for a purpose. Please show me my purpose in life and guide me on my path today."

• • •

5

Dating: A Cautionary Tale

All discarded lovers should be given a second chance,
but with somebody else.

— MAE WEST

For the alcoholic single mother, the dos and don'ts of dating are convoluted and complex. Dating for anyone today is like a minefield, but for recovering women, especially recovering moms who already have a history of disastrous relationships, the dangers are even greater. My friend Diane told me, "I've dated every dysfunctional man in Arizona, so I had to move to California." You may feel like your Prize Picker is totally broken after so many failed attempts, or maybe you had no relationships and just slept around, looking for love in all the wrong places. You may be the woman who never dated and had given up on ever finding love.

It was suggested I refrain from dating for the first year in sobriety, which I thought was absurd. I put down the drink and picked up the men (plural). The first one was thirty days sober and I was ninety days sober. It was love at first sight: my dysfunction was attracted to his dysfunction—a perfect fit.

My next victim, like me, had three young kids. What a recipe for disaster! We were both under a year sober and had six kids under the age of ten; someone should have had me committed. As I heard in a meeting, "I should have been committed for some of the things I was committed to." Thank God we never got as far as moving in together: After we broke up he started dating a woman I knew, and much later when she and I became friends, she revealed that he was a porn addict.

My worst horror story happened when I was ten years sober and thinking I was doing everything right. I broke the cardinal rule and dated a newcomer to recovery, ignoring every red flag. (As a Southern friend of mine said, "When you see red flags, it doesn't mean a parade is coming to town.") He told me he was divorced and I soon found out he was actually just separated, not to mention he'd lost his house and had no job or car. So what does a good alcoholic woman do? I moved him in with my kids. Ugh! I waited desperately for two years for him to end his marriage to his not-so-ex-wife. I finally set a bottom line and told him to move out and not call me until he was fully divorced. Soon after this, I got a collect call from the Fresno jail after he had gotten his fourth DUI. I did not bail him out. That night I called his wife and told her he was in jail. During the conversation my sick mind could not help but ask if they had slept together while he'd been living with me. I was sure she'd say no, but of course she said yes.

I finally realized that this desperate search for love through multiple dysfunctional relationships was a pattern that signaled I had developed another addiction besides alcoholism, and I was getting sicker and sicker. One of my biggest fears had been that I'd drink if my heart got broken. But I hadn't even thought of drinking during any of these crises. I simply went on to the next unmanageable relationship, violating my standards faster than I could lower them. But with this one, I'd finally hit my bottom. I went to Sex and Love Addicts Anonymous (SLAA) to address my love addiction, and thus began a new journey in recovery.

Instead of taking a year off from dating, as my first AA sponsors had suggested, I decided to take two years off to work the Steps in SLAA. I realized I was that sick. I vowed to never disappoint myself again in my choice of men.

After I took the two years off, my SLAA sponsor suggested I make a list of the qualities I wanted in a partner. So I started with a list for my dream man. My list included:

- financially successful and responsible
- honest and trustworthy
- good-looking
- fun-loving, good sense of humor
- warm, generous, emotionally available
- able to adore all of my children and me

Of course, I didn't believe at the time that any of this was possible. Because my self-esteem was so low I didn't think a man with these qualities would be interested in me. I showed the list to my sponsor, hoping she would give me her blessing. Instead, she told me to become the person with all the qualities on my list, and then I'd attract the man I wanted.

After fifteen years of intense work on myself—working the Twelve Steps (including making many amends and praying like hell as I searched for my Higher Power), getting a lot of therapy, showing up for work every day, and learning to laugh at myself—I *have* become the person I wanted to be, at least most of the time. Today I know that I deserve a partner with these qualities, and I'm no longer willing to settle for anything less.

Sober Mom's Tools for Healthy Dating

1. Make a list of the qualities you want in a partner. Now work on becoming the person on your list!

2. Dating prayer: "Higher Self, help me feel your love, and help me love myself as well. I know you made me lovable exactly the way I am, and I don't have to be anyone other than who you made me to be. Help me heal the wounds of the past, when I believed that I didn't deserve love. Surround me with safe, loving people, and if it is your will for me to find a life partner, lead me to the person you have chosen for me."

3. Enlist a friend you trust to be your dating coach, and be honest with her. When there are red flags in a relationship, ask her to remind you that the parade isn't coming to town—it's time to step back and take a hard look at what you're doing. She might also need to remind you to keep your pants on!

4. If your children are under eighteen years old, commit to a friend, sponsor, or dating coach to hold you accountable to *not* introduce the person you are dating to your children until you two have been dating for a year and you have both committed to each other.

• • •

6

Money Money Money

A woman's best protection is a little money of her own.
— CLARE BOOTHE LUCE

Two of the biggest relapse triggers I see with my clients and sponsees are romance and finance. As addicts and alcoholics, most of us have money issues. Just as we learn to have healthy relationships with people, we also need to learn to have a healthy relationship with money. Most people would rather tell you their deepest, darkest secrets or about their sex life than tell you about their dysfunctional relationship with money.

My relationship with money was definitely dysfunctional! When I was married I often went mindlessly shopping for clothes, shoes, you name it, and hid the bags from my husband. He'd ask me, "Is that new?" and I'd reply, "I've had this for ages—you just never notice." I often padded the grocery bill and I even stole money from the kids' piggy banks.

When I was about five years sober, I hit my bottom with money. I was $60,000 in debt and I could hardly breathe. I was a single mom trying to raise three children in a very expensive area. I made good money but I could never seem to save—I always spent more money than I had. I was so ashamed, embarrassed, and filled with fear. I was afraid to open bills. I lay awake nights worrying about money. Many days I wanted to drink because I was so uncomfortable. I was almost at the point of hopelessness, and then I ran into a woman named Terri D., who I knew through AA. When she asked me how I was doing, I broke down in tears and told her the truth. It was then she shared her recovery story with me.

She told me how she realized that much of her unhappiness had to do with her fear of economic insecurity, as identified in the Big Book of AA in its section on the Fourth Step. She made me laugh: when she shared in her first Debtors Anonymous meeting that she was afraid of becoming a bag lady, a fellow in the program said, "Maybe a Gucci bag lady." Terri D. identified herself as an under-earner and began taking steps to understand and improve her relationship with money. I didn't relate to that part, because I was always able to earn a really good income. But I did relate to her inability to save money and take good care of herself financially. She mentioned that her struggles were a reflection of her low self-esteem and immaturity. Yuck! I didn't want to admit to that at all, yet I knew it was true.

Her comment pierced a hole in the lie I was displaying to the world—the lie that I had it all together because I looked good and drove a fancy car. My fancy red BMW had been an impulse buy that I couldn't afford. I'd even gotten a vanity license plate: ROSES R RED. Terri D. told me how she acquired some practical tools that, later on, sustained and supported her husband while he was in school and they had two children in diapers. This comment burst a hole in my fantasy of waiting for a wealthy man to come rescue me from my money troubles. She suggested I try a Debtors Anonymous (DA) meeting. "Oh, good God," I thought, "Not another Twelve Step meeting." I was already doing AA and Al-Anon, yet I was in so much fear that I decided to take her suggestion.

The first step I learned was to track my spending and earning. I needed this not only to gain clarity about where my money was going, but to start becoming aware of my relationship to money. The next step was to create a spending plan, which allowed me to make better choices with my money: choices that reflected my values, goals, and dreams.

When I went to my first DA meeting, I met people who had been where I was now, and it helped lessen the shame. It was that day I committed to get out of debt. That commitment was put to the test when I was out of work for four months and my vacuum cleaner broke. I had three kids, a not-so-white carpet, and no vacuum. My first instinct was to run out and charge a new one on a credit card, then I remembered the promise I'd made to myself about not debiting. I grabbed my little dust buster and got down on my hands and knees to vacuum up all the crumbs.

As I vacuumed, I felt pity for myself, but since that didn't make the situation any better I decided to try the gratitude prayer. I thanked God for the crumbs because it meant we had food to eat. I said thank you for the carpet, and the table the food fell from, all of which were housed in a beautiful home for my kids and me. I thanked God for the three wonderful healthy children who had probably dropped the crumbs. I suddenly found myself weeping with gratitude for all the blessings in my life. I realized all these gifts were from God, and all I needed to do was trust. Oh, and to continue dust-busting the thousand other crumbs as well!

A sponsee of mine had lost her job and was overwhelmed with the bills that were stacking up. She was so paralyzed she couldn't even open the bills; she threw them in a bag so they were out of her sight. She wasn't sleeping at night because she was worried about how she was going to feed her kids. I reminded her there was food in the refrigerator, a roof over her head, and gas in the car. No one was knocking on the door to evict her or repo her car today. I told her to bring the bag of bills to my house. We balanced her checkbook and we figured out all her minimum needs. With clarity on the amount of money she had and the money she needed to cover the basic needs of food, rent, and gas, she felt less overwhelmed. Then we opened one bill at a time. We made one pile of the bills she could pay now, making sure she had enough first for her basic needs for the next thirty days. She wrote a few checks and put them in the mail. The second pile was for the bills she couldn't pay now. We called the creditors and let them know she'd lost her job and that her intention was to pay, but for now she could only pay them five dollars a month. While most of the creditors weren't happy, I told my sponsee that she wasn't doing this to please them, she was doing it for her self-esteem and to face reality.

I then asked her how much money she'd realistically like to make in her next job. She gave me the number, and I had her add ten percent to it, because most of us underestimate our value and worth. Then I suggested to her that it was now her full-time job to find a job. She would need to be at her desk at eight in the morning. She could take a lunch break from noon to one, then get back to work until five, when she could stop for the day and let her Higher Power go to work for her. I told her to do this five days a week until she found a job. I also suggested she send her resume to everyone she knew and all her past clients, hand-deliver her resume into the companies, pray like hell, and ignore people who say the job market is awful.

When she got an interview, I told her to follow up with a hand-written thank-you letter with three letters of recommendation through FedEx. If she hadn't heard from the employer in a week, she should call to see if the job had been filled and, if

MONEY MONEY MONEY | 31

not, to remind them she's very interested. I'm pleased to say my sponsee found a job that paid her 25 percent more than her last job and gave her a step up in her career.

When I decided to leave a stable career and a steady paycheck to open my own business, I had to listen to my own suggestions—the ones I'd given my clients and sponsees. I, too, had to ask for help, take one step at a time, and pray like hell. I called Terri D., who had introduced me to DA years before, because I knew she was running her own successful business as a financial coach. I hired her right away because I knew that with her help my business was sure to be a success. Today I still work with Terri D. as my business grows, evolves, and continues to be a success.

When we face our fears, get out of our head, and take action, things can start to fall into place and we feel empowered. If we don't beat ourselves up and take care of business, we can feel good about ourselves. When I pay my bills on time with gratitude, I am in right relationship with my money. I don't worship, obsess, or undervalue money. I believe my Higher Power wants me to have freedom and abundance with money as She does in all my relationships.

Vagueness about money keeps me in fear. When I balance my checkbook and keep track of my expenses I feel free. When I go on wild spending sprees I feel guilty and out of control.

I have learned that my worth is not connected to my wallet, the clothes I wear, or the car I drive. We are all worthy. According to one dictionary, *worth* is "usefulness or importance, as to the world, to a person, or for a purpose." My worth today is more about giving than getting. As the Big Book of AA says, "We must be careful not to drift into worry, remorse or morbid reflection, for that would diminish our usefulness to others" (page 86). I learned my fears are never about the money.

Regardless of how much money I had or did not have, the hole I was trying to fill was the feeling that " I am not enough." A mantra I learned was "I have enough, I do enough, and I am enough."

The hole I have tried to fill with ever-more *stuff* is a bottomless pit. When I am spiritually fit and useful to others, that deep, dark pit is filled with a feeling of purpose and usefulness to others. Today I do my best to show up for work, pay my bills on time, save money, donate to charities, and remember to be grateful for my sobriety and all the abundance in my life.

Sober Mom's Tools for Financial Recovery

1. Make a spending plan: Ask a trusted friend who is good with money to help you create a budget and get your financial affairs in order. Remember: once you take the monster of fear of financial insecurity out of the closet, it loses its power.

2. Open a savings account: Put a little in every month, even if it's only five dollars; a small amount still builds your self-esteem. If you get unexpected money, put it into savings, instead of your checking account.

3. For a month, write down each day what you purchased and the amount you spent. This will give you greater clarity about your relationship with money.

4. Expect a miracle: When I'm conscious about my finances and taking care of business, I notice that the money I need will be available, often unexpectedly.

• • •

7

Intimacy: Into Me You See

Fear is the great enemy of intimacy.
Fear makes us run away from each other or
cling to each other but does not create true intimacy.

— HENRI NOUWEN

Intimacy is one of the greatest human needs—that longing for someone to truly, deeply know and accept us for who we truly are. We all have a primal human desire to connect with another person on a deep spiritual and emotional level, a yearning to be known and understood. We want to know that we matter, that our presence on this planet has a purpose. As mothers we can provide this for our children.

Before I got sober, I had the false expectation that this yearning for intimacy was fulfilled through having sex. As my friend Diane said, "We go to bed with a man, and the next morning he's planning golf while we're shopping for the wedding dress."

Another fallacy I believed was that if I had a man in my life, it would mean I did matter; I would never feel afraid, lost, or unsettled. I knew nothing about healthy emotional closeness. I was afraid that if a man really knew me, he wouldn't accept me. I had sex with many men thinking it would bond us, but they obviously didn't get my memo. I thought it was my job to please them sexually, and if I didn't they might leave me for another woman. It took me a long time and a lot of pain to find out how wrong I was.

I also thought intimacy was just reserved for a partner. I had no idea what it was like to be intimate with my children. For children to develop a healthy sense of self, they need a mother who is emotionally present. Although I was physically present, I was not emotionally present. There is an innate bond between a mother and child, and nothing breaks that bond faster than addiction. In the thrall of my addictions I was an emotional wreck. In sobriety I learned to be present with my children so they developed a healthy sense of self-worth and stability.

Many couples struggle with intimacy and need therapy to discover their intimacy blocks. Two obvious blocks are infidelity and addictions. Other blocks, which can hide beneath the surface, are low self-esteem, unresolved anger, fear of being hurt, and unrealistic expectations. It takes trust and commitment to be willing to face these issues, especially if they have been denied or avoided for a long time. Since most addicts and alcoholics come into Twelve Step programs with low self-esteem and unresolved anger, it can take years to work through intimacy issues. Many women have been sexually abused, and physical intimacy can be challenging if this trauma is not healed. (More about this later.) A woman I know was making love to her husband when all of the sudden she had a flashback of being sexually molested. She jumped out of bed and started having a panic attack. It took awhile for her to discuss this with her husband because of her shame. Needless to say she was unable to be sexually intimate with her husband until she had worked with a therapist around this trauma. Her husband was compassionate and understanding. She eventually came to understand her primary need to feel emotionally connected in order to be sexually intimate with her husband.

Most children are watching their parents navigate their relationship. It is important for the parents to model basic healthy relationship skills, such as demonstrating caring and affection, respecting each other as separate individuals, accepting each other's imperfections and forgiving mistakes, spending quality time with each other, and maintaining open communication that includes listening.

For me, intimacy means I can be honest with the other person and be myself. I don't have to pretend to be someone I'm not so they will accept me. I can reveal my true self—the good, the bad, and the ugly parts of me—to a person with whom I've established the trust that is essential to intimacy. I have learned that it's important to "say what I mean, mean what I say, and don't say it mean."

I don't have to twist myself into a pretzel to be who I think you want me to be. That's what I did when I was ninety days sober and pretending to have it all together. People would ask, "How are you doing?" I'd respond with a big fake smile and say, "I'm fine," even as I was going through a divorce; trying to raise three young kids; filled with guilt, pain, and fear; and wanting to drink every moment of the day. I certainly was not *fine* unless you mean the acronym: a f***ed-up, insecure, neurotic, emotional mess.

Finally, one day I was sitting in a meeting and I just couldn't fake it anymore. I burst into tears and fell apart, desperately asking for help. This was the true beginning of my recovery. I remember a wonderful old man named Eddie (God rest his soul) who I'd see at the AA Club House every day. Day after day he looked me straight in the eye and told me I was a beautiful person. Most days I would disregard his comment, dismissing him with a thank-you. Yet this day I broke down in tears and said to Eddie, "I can't wait until the day I actually feel that way about myself." Eddie reassured me that if I continued to work the Twelve Steps of Alcoholics Anonymous I would soon feel beautiful inside and out.

Revealing my authentic self allowed people to truly know me and love me, warts and all. Revealing myself while not being judged by others was the beginning of my compassion for myself.

The first time I felt really known and seen was when I did my first Fourth Step with my sponsor. I revealed all the fears, resentments, harms, and hurts from my drinking days and before—all the feelings and secrets I had stuffed and was afraid to tell anyone. She opened up to me and revealed that one of my deepest, darkest secrets was something she'd experienced, too. She did not judge me, and I felt our spirits connect. She saw into me—all the suffering, loneliness, and shame. I realized that here was a woman who no longer carried that shame and was at peace with her past. Because of the "sin" I had committed, I thought God would want nothing to do with me, and I surely would never be able to forgive myself. She said, "Rosemary, your Higher Power has already forgiven you. It's time to let go of your past and forgive yourself."

Being able to trust another woman opened the floodgates to let all that shame and anger out. Healing began, and I could feel my spirit again. I pictured a chalkboard with the slate wiped clean, my past erased: I was given a whole new life. Today I am no longer an empty cup, running from person to person begging each one to fill my cup with acceptance and love. Today I fill that cup with God's love, and I have learned how to love myself, like myself, respect myself, and forgive myself. I'm able to bring my whole self to my relationships, and that allows me to give and receive healthy love. This is intimacy.

Sober Mom's Tools for Finding Intimacy

1. Share your story, including the shame and the secrets, with a trusted sponsor or friend who has at least two years of sobriety and who is working a solid Twelve Step program.

2. After you have completed all Twelve Steps, become a sponsor. Then you will have the privilege of sharing your experience of intimacy with other women by sharing your story and hearing her story.

3. Look at yourself in the mirror every day and say out loud, "I am worthy of love, respect, and forgiveness."

4. If you are in a committed relationship with a partner and are having intimacy problems, seek help from a therapist who has the credentials and experience for working with couples on relationship issues. Learn what your blocks to intimacy are, and work with the therapist to heal them.

5. If your relationship and intimacy issues include your children, seek out a respected family therapist and involve the whole family.

• • •

8

Are You a Drama Mama?

Drama doesn't just walk into your life out of nowhere;
you create it, invite it, or associate with people who bring it.
— ANONYMOUS

When I was drinking and using, everything was a drama, mostly because I caused the drama-producing situation in the first place. We put on the costume of victim or wronged party. We put on the tiara of righteousness and we waved our queen wand, pointing it at others who we insisted had harmed us. Our princess gown was of course white because we were such angels. Woe is me.

When we're going into Drama Mama mode, we make everything a big deal. We make up stories that have little to do with reality. We get everyone on our side. We get hysterical about our situation and build a big drama around it. By the time we've told the fifth friend our tale of woe, it's become an epic movie starring us.

This drama behavior can become really unhealthy and damaging to the kids, especially if the drama involves the other parent. If you say things in front of the children like "Your dad's an idiot—he doesn't give us enough money, and don't you think his new girlfriend looks cheap?" the child feels like a ping-pong ball, always being forced to take sides.

Being in Drama Mama mode causes a kind of adrenaline rush similar to the rush from a drink or drug, and it makes us feel powerful, even if we're hurt or upset. During one of my pregnancies, an acquaintance said, "Oh, I forget you're pregnant until I see how fat your face is." Then she laughed. Instead of telling her that the remark had hurt my feelings and it wasn't okay to talk to me like that, I stewed with resentment and phoned five friends to perpetuate my wounded-victim feelings. I didn't know how to speak up for myself and often expected my husband to stand up and rescue me. I've learned in recovery that it's up to me to let people know how I want to be treated, instead of using drama to get my feelings out. I found my voice in recovery and have learned how to handle situations that used to baffle me. I replaced the drama with honesty and self-respect.

My life got a lot simpler when I took off the Drama Mama costume around my children and other mothers. Before, I easily got indignant about kids who didn't treat my children right. If another kid wronged my kid, I would get on the phone and ask the other mothers, "How could Mary let her child treat my kid that way?"

When my daughter was the only one who wasn't invited to a school birthday party, I was more hurt than my daughter was. I called all the other mothers in the classroom and told them indignantly what a horrible parent that mother was to not invite my child. In my head I planned my revenge; later I'd throw an extravagant party and invite the entire school except her daughter. I glared at the woman every time I saw her and even fantasized about tripping the birthday girl on the playground. After my daughter heard me complaining yet again to a friend about how unfair this was, she came in the room and said, "Mom, it's okay. I don't like the girl, and I don't want to even go to the party."

In recovery we learn how exhausting it is to keep creating drama in our lives, and we become willing to change. We learn that when our actions are driven by self-will, our life is a soap opera and we play all the roles. To stop the drama we learn to stop blowing every little thing out of proportion. We learn that we don't have to "attach" to everything that happens like a blood-sucking vampire, that we can actually let go and trust our Higher Power. What a concept!

The deepest spiritual work around the Drama Mama syndrome is to recognize that "when I'm hysterical, it's historical." Most of our current upsets can be traced back to old wounds that we bring into current situations. In recovery we learn to pause when upset and ask for the right thought or action. We let go in the moment and don't add fuel to the fire. Our longstanding wounds, repressed emotions, and resentments will be revealed and healed in doing the Fourth and Fifth inventory steps.

To defuse the Drama Mama mode, we need to change our thinking and our behavior, which begins with working Steps Six through Twelve. Step Ten especially gives us a tool for promptly dealing with our harmful behaviors. We also can depend on the support of our Twelve Step group: when we catch ourselves wanting to call someone to bitch and moan about the current situation, we instead call our sponsor, who will help us defuse the drama and guide us to finding a solution to the problem that caused the upset. We commence to outgrow our Drama Mama tendencies and are able to create a calmer and more serene environment for our children.

Sober Mom's Tools
to Overcome Being a Drama Mama

1. Stop! Stop in the name of love—think it over! Sometimes all we need to do about the Drama Mama reaction is to just stop,

pause, back off. You might ask yourself, *Is being upset worth ruining my day (or several days), or can I just make a decision to let go?* Then turn your attention to something positive. Call a friend or somebody from your Twelve Step group, and don't relive the problem. It will be hard at first, but then it will become a relief to let go of the drama.

2. When disturbed, take a spot-check written inventory—there is magic in getting your upset out of your head and down on paper. We frequently find out how we are actually feeling by writing about it. Writing your thoughts and feelings down is a tool that will become your best ally. Ask yourself, *Why am I upset? What is the core fear under my discomfort?*

3. Ask yourself, *What can I do differently? Did I place myself in a position to be hurt?* You will often feel real freedom by finding the answers to these questions, and you can learn a lot about what makes you tick.

4. Defuse situations instead of pouring gasoline on them and striking a match! Just for today, de-stress, de-drama, and be a Mellow Mama.

5. If you haven't already done it, do a Fourth Step, then make an appointment to meet with your sponsor and do your Fifth Step.

6. Prayer: "God, I know you are here with me now. Calm my fears and let me know everything is okay. Send me warm, caring people to comfort me in these times. I know you are showing me what needs to be healed in this situation. Help me to be compassionate and to be present for my children."

. . .

9

Love Relationship Dysfunction

My fear of abandonment is exceeded only by
my terror of intimacy.

— ETHLIE ANN VARE

In the rooms of AA, it's suggested that we not date for the first year because we need that time to focus on our recovery. Often we see women replace their obsession with alcohol and other drugs with a craving for an intimate partner; sometimes they'll even put their children second to satisfying this need. We need to remember as mothers in recovery that our primary goal now is to stay sober and create a stable and safe environment for our children. The last thing our children need is for their newly sober mothers to switch their focus to a new love interest or to have a stranger invade their environment. Not only does this behavior take us away from our children, it often leads to relapse.

When I put down the alcohol, I picked up a man. My sponsor tried to warn me against having a relationship that soon. But I thought those guidelines didn't apply to me: I was different and could handle it. To make her point, she had me stand up and do the pillow exercise. She stuck one pillow under my right arm and said, "This pillow symbolizes your recovery." She then put three more pillows under my left arm and said, "These represent your children." Finally, she put one last pillow under my chin and said it represented my full-time job. As I stood there awkwardly, she gave the final instruction: "Now reach out and hug your new boyfriend." Of course when I reached out my arms, all the pillows dropped. It was a rude awakening, clearly illustrating that bringing a man into my life at this point would lead me to drop everything else that was important to me. Yet even with all this evidence, I didn't take her advice.

So when I was ninety days sober, I got involved with Mr. Thirty-Days-Sober. Boy, was this dysfunction junction. Soon I was complaining to a friend that I was paying for everything because my new boyfriend did not have a job. I felt bad for grumbling, though, thinking that perhaps I was being too hard on him.

This wise woman said to me, "Rosemary, being employed is right up there with taking a shower daily. You are not being too hard on him; you are just lowering your standards. Paying for everything is not good for you or him. If you are in a relationship with a man and want to change everything about him, then you have no right to be in the relationship." As we continued talking, my friend asked me, "Is this a man you would want your daughter to date when she grows up?" Wow, that thought woke me up like a cold bucket of ice. As a mother in recovery, I need to consider what my behavior is modeling for my children. Though most of us learn about relationships from Hollywood and the media—including many untruths, such as *You're not enough without a better half* and *Your knight in shining armor is on his way to rescue you*—our children are not only watching television, movies, and listening to love songs, they are watching *you*. Ask yourself, *Is this what I'd want for my child?*

Of course it is normal to want love and romance in our lives. But when the pursuit of love and romance becomes compulsive and turns to obsession—we need the "hit" of being with this person—then it is another form of addiction, known as a love addiction. And as with a chemical addiction, the consequences of this addiction can be devastating. It can ruin marriages, kill self-esteem, and even lead to suicide.

Love addiction often begins in early childhood due to lack of healthy bonding with the primary caregiver. Love addicts have a strong fear of abandonment, which often stems from rejection, neglect, or abuse—physical, emotional, or sexual—in early childhood. The core driving need for love addicts is re-assurance from the love object. Love addicts need someone to tell them they are okay and are lovable, desirable, and worthy because they don't believe it about themselves. Love addiction can be an escape from reality, loneliness, and stress and a way to avoid true intimacy.

Some common signs of a love addict:

- compulsively fantasizing about, or focusing on, one person
- becoming attracted to emotionally unavailable or abusive partners
- moving quickly from one relationship to another
- feeling incomplete without a partner
- neglecting to care for self
- becoming sexually or emotionally involved without knowing the other person
- wanting to be rescued to avoid taking responsibility for ourselves

Love addiction takes different forms: there's Sandy the serial dater, Candy the cling-on, Francis the fantasy queen. Then we have Alice the avoider who dates married men or men who are not emotionally available. Amber is a relationship anorexic who has given up on relationships and hasn't gone out on a date in years. All of these behaviors come from a place of fear of abandonment, rejection, and/or feeling as if you are not enough.

I have shown up in most of these roles in my own love addiction. For example, when I was a little girl, Francis the fantasy queen was very prevalent. I often fantasized that my prince in shining armor would come whisk me away to happily ever after. Little girls who don't feel safe and are not getting loving attention from their parents feel abandoned, so they may look for someone else to fulfill this need. In recovery we find a way to heal this sense of abandonment.

The main role I played in my love addiction was Sandy the serial dater. I would spot a man, beeline to him, flirt up a storm, and if he gave me even the slightest bit of attention I was hooked. The shelf lives of these relationships were one to three months. I played instant girlfriend, lover, cook, sponsor, psychiatrist, banker, and job counselor. One day I'd be saying "I love you," and the next day, out of the blue, I was saying goodbye. After I was exhausted from these fixer-uppers who weren't working out as well as I'd hoped, I'd move on to the next victim. I thought it was my partner's job to make me feel lovable. Again, I was going from man to man with an empty, bottomless cup, begging for love and attention. It was never enough because I didn't feel enough.

Then my pattern unexpectedly broke. I became friends with a man who had previously dated one of my sponsees. When she broke up with him he cried on my shoulder and I listened and "comforted" him. We became intimate, he took me on a fabulous trip, bought me roses, cooked me dinner, showered me with attention, and then bang, the voicemail: "I'm getting back together with my ex-girlfriend." News flash: I suddenly realized that he'd done to me what I had done to a string of men.

What makes me cringe the most is how my serial dating affected my children. They witnessed the revolving door. If you don't think your children are paying attention, it's proof that you are checked out. I'd spend hours on the phone with the man of the moment. My five-year-old son would try to pull me away from the phone, and I'd tell him to go watch TV. He needed me. Although I was physically present at home, I was emotionally checked out. I chose time on the phone over being present with my children. I chose dates over my kids' sporting events. Basically, I chose men over my children more times than I care to admit. Just as I had formerly used alcohol, I was now using men to escape from the pressures of parenting, work, and running a household. My plate was full, and I was scared, exhausted, and overwhelmed. Not for the first time, I thought a man could rescue me. I thought the problem with my marriage was I'd chosen the wrong man. In my serial dating I was trying to find the right man so I could put together the perfect little family and my happy-ever-after fantasy.

When I started my journey in recovering from dysfunctional love relationships, the women in the meeting rooms held my hand and taught me how to be present for my children. One night I called a friend from the program, complaining about having to do this and that for my kids. It was early evening and there was dinner to be made, homework to be supervised, dishes to be washed, laundry to be done, and three cranky children who needed me. I told the women I was going to run to my second AA meeting of the day. She asked if there was some chance I was trying to escape from my responsibilities as a mother. Was I running to a meeting hoping to see the man I had a crush on? Ugh, I was busted.

She suggested that instead I take a hot bubble bath, forget the dishes and laundry for the day, turn off my phone, order a pizza, and sit down with the kids and ask them how their days were. Another great suggestion she had was to tell my kids we could all snuggle and watch TV together for a half hour if they finished their homework on time. After I tucked them all in bed that night and climbed into my own bed, I felt so good about myself as a mother and the rewards of being present for my children. I recognized this was much better than any "hit" I could have received from seeing any man.

Over that same year, I had witnessed one of my best friends in recovery struggle with love addiction. This was a beautiful, spirited, present woman until she became obsessed with her new boyfriend and his porn addiction. As she progressed in her love addiction, the light faded from her spirit and nearly went out. When I was with her during this time, she was elsewhere, completely checked out as if in some sort of trance. One day she actually called him twenty-three times and when he still didn't answer, she left her young children home alone and drove to his house in the middle of the night to peer into his window. When she started her recovery from love addition, I saw her beautiful light return and her spirit come alive again. When I received that voicemail telling me I was being dumped, she reached her hand out and took me to my first Twelve Step meeting of Sex and Love Addicts Anonymous. I was so angry to be there, I raised my hand and blurted, "You all better promise me the man of my dreams if I do this program." I didn't know at the time that the program had nothing to do with finding a romantic partner.

When I starting working the Twelve Steps in SLAA with a sponsor she, too, suggested I take a year off from dating and pay attention to all the ways I seek attention from men. I didn't think I was doing anything to seek attention, but I agreed to try it anyway.

One morning soon after, I got dressed for the gym in my usual attire: tight biking shorts and low-cut workout top. At the gym, I got on the stair climber (a machine that assured all the men were watching and counting every step I took) and started scanning the room, looking for a man to make eye contact with. For whatever reason I didn't get any man's attention that day—no "hits"—and I ran out of the gym crying hysterically. At that moment, I realized part of my draw to the gym was the attention I received from men. When I told my sponsor about it, she recommended I quit the gym—and stop working out with my hot-guy trainer as well. The sessions I spent with my trainer twice a week made me feel special; he gave me his undivided attention for an entire hour! But now I realized I was using him to get my hits.

Before recovery from love addiction, I did all kinds of things to get a man to notice me. I laugh now at all the ways I tried to reel a man in. I'd try to figure out what my partner wanted me to be, and then play that role. I did this so often that I had no idea who I really was. Case in point: once I was dating a very conservative man who wore plaid shorts and polo shirts. I was going to meet his family so I bought a pair of plaid pants, a polo shirt, and cute little pink loafers to match, hoping to fit in. Boy, did my friends get a kick out of how ridiculous I looked. They knew as well as I did that I was not comfortable in this outfit.

Another time I had a crush on a man who was into mountain biking. Trying to do anything to spend time with him, I told him I was into mountain biking too. He asked me to go biking the next day. I ran right out and bought a bike, new outfit, biking shoes, gloves, water bottle, and a god-awful biking helmet that ruined my beautifully washed and styled hair.

In recovery, I've learned that I don't have to buy stupid,

expensive outfits to please someone else. I now please *me* and I know who I am. I've learned again that my addiction is not about the drink, the drug, or the guy; recovery is about healing the core belief that tells me I'm not enough. This feeling of *I'm not enough* is a lie that haunts most women with addictions. It drives us to continually seek more, more, more love, confirmation of our worth, and approval from others. Instead of finding the man of my dreams, what I found was a wonderful woman who was hiding deep inside; I found me, the real me! I learned to love and respect myself. I discovered a deep feeling and knowing that I am lovable and I am *enough*. Warts and all! As a friend once told me, "I may not be perfect, but parts of me are excellent!"

Sober Mom's Tools
for Overcoming Love Addiction

1. Regularly attend one of these Twelve Step meeting groups: Love Addicts Anonymous (LAA) or Sex and Love Addicts Anonymous (SLAA). I recommend you go to all-women meetings for the first year.

2. Visit the Sex and Love Addicts Anonymous site (slaafws.org) and complete the "40 Questions for Self-diagnosis" (found under the tab *Is SLAA for me?*). Go to CODA.org and read "Characteristics of a Co-dependent." Both of these Twelve Step programs can change your relationship dysfunction.

3. Find a therapist who specializes in love addiction and commit to seeing that person for a year to work on this issue.

4. Take a year off from dating, flirting, and dressing sexy. (This is not about you becoming a nun. It's about learning to value you instead of getting "hits" from someone else.)

5. While you are taking a year off from dating (or try one month at a time) treat yourself as you would like a partner to treat you. Make yourself a dinner as if you were having a date over. (You can also have "dates" with your children from time to time.) Set the table with your nice dishes, light the candles, cook a beautiful meal, and actually sit down for at least fifteen minutes and eat it. Buy yourself flowers, write a love letter to yourself, take yourself to the movies, buy yourself a special gift, take yourself for a night away and each day say the words you are longing to hear from a partner, such as "You are so beautiful and I love you so much." If you think about something you would like a partner to do for you, then do it for yourself.

6. Work on your own personal growth and developing your talents. Work on improving your relationship with your children.

• • •

10

Supermom

I'd like to be the ideal mother,
but I'm too busy raising my kids.

— ANONYMOUS

The baby is crying, the dog is barking, your husband is snoring, and you look over at the clock and realize you went to bed just five hours ago. You grab the baby, let the dog out, and sleepwalk to the coffee pot. The dishes from the night before are still piled high in the sink, and you're out of formula for the baby. You run to the store to grab some formula, still in your slippers with a coat on to hide your pajamas. By the time you get back home, the other kids are demanding breakfast. You pour them some cereal, pack their lunches, and hurry them to the car because you're late once again to drive the car pool to school and daycare. Oh, and you're still in your pajamas!

You arrive home and finally pour yourself that first cup of coffee. Now your husband wakes up from his restful night of sleep and is so glad you're home for a little hanky-panky. "You've got to be kidding me!" you shriek. He looks at you in wonder, as if he can't figure out why you're never in the mood. He turns and sulks off toward the shower, but calls out to see if you wouldn't mind ironing his shirt and bringing him a cup of coffee because he is running a bit late. It's eight fifteen and you're already exhausted. Your husband kisses you good-bye, flies out the door, and says he'll be home late tonight. As you run upstairs to take your own shower, the phone rings; it's your daughter calling from school to tell you she's forgotten her lunch. Suddenly you remember you have to be at work on time for a presentation, one that you'd planned to finish preparing last night. Now you definitely have no time for a shower.

Does this scene sound familiar to you? It's someone trying to be a Supermom—running around like a basket case with an endless to-do list trying to please everyone and ending up frazzled and exhausted.

Before recovery, this was my life. I wanted to do it all: be the perfect mom, the perfect wife, the perfect employee. I wanted to live the picture-perfect Christmas-card life. Everything needed to look good on the outside. The house had to be spotless, like a model home where no one actually lived. The outfits my children wore were matching and of the latest fashion. My body needed to be perfectly toned and slim. Trying to keep up with the Joneses (whoever the hell they are) was exhausting and unachievable—and it conflicted with my recovery program and principles.

Over the years I've seen many other women—my clients, sponsees, and friends—fly around town in their own Supermom capes. One client told me about her nonstop schedule, which began at six when she got up to prepare breakfast for her family, and ended at eleven at night, when the kids were in bed, the dishes done, and the house was spotless again. She also worked six days a week. I asked what she did on her day off. She laughed and said it was spent preparing for the next week—doing laundry, grocery shopping, and attending to *all* the other details she didn't have time to do during the week. I mistakenly asked her what her husband did to help out. Without batting an eye she told me he doesn't help out at all. She said in the past she would ask him to help, but he never did. Tired of always being disappointed, she stopped asking.

I felt the hurt and disappointment in her voice, so I decided to pause and we sat in silence for a while. Then the tears started streaming down her face. I could see that she was trying to hold them back, but I encouraged her to just let the tears flow. My mom once told me that tears are the angels washing the pain away. I continued to sit with her for about five minutes while she sobbed. We ended that session together by her committing to hire a house cleaner twice a month. Yet her real takeaway was realizing *why* she was running at such a fast pace and overdoing everything: so she didn't have to feel disappointment. I have witnessed many mothers (including myself) fly around in the Supermom cape at speeds faster than lightning so we don't have to stop and feel the feelings of *not being enough*. I teach my clients this mantra: "I have enough, I do enough, and I am enough."

We often don't stop to realize the impact our Supermom role has on our children. Not only do they grow up believing that moms must do it all, but most kids these days are overscheduled themselves, pulled from one place to another. They're up at six thirty in the morning, attend school all day, and then run from piano lessons to soccer until dark. When these kids finally arrive home, they need to start their three hours of homework. It's no wonder our kids are stressed out, exhausted, and cranky—just like their mothers—or that they, too, turn to alcohol and drugs.

Then there are the single moms who do all the above without a partner to offer any help or financial support. The single moms who co-parent have the added stress of coordinating their children's care with the other parent.

Many mothers are taking the "mommy's little secret" drug,

Adderall (or some other stimulant), just so they can accomplish everything they think *must* be done. One mother of four children described how she'd take a handful of Adderall so she could stay up until two in the morning to clean the house and do all the laundry. She thought it was the greatest thing since sliced bread—until she went from using Adderall to smoking meth. When her thirteen-year-old daughter caught her smoking meth in the garage at one in the morning, she knew it was time to get help. All of this happened in a luxurious home overlooking the ocean in sunny Southern California.

Another mother I was trying to help would wake up and take Xanax all day long so she could deal with the stress, and Ambien each night so she could sleep. She thought this was normal behavior because all the moms in her child's play group were doing it. Unfortunately she wasn't one of the lucky ones. Neither were her children, as they lost their mom to an overdose. Trying to do it all can literally kill us.

Oh, what a relief when I finally surrendered my Superwoman cape. It was so exhausting to be everything to everyone and *no one to myself.* Often we moms never make it onto our own to-do list, putting everyone else's needs before our own, including our basic needs like food, sleep, and hygiene. I was actually quite shocked when I surrendered the cape and the world didn't fall apart without me. It was a relief and a disappointment at the same time.

I remember one evening when my former husband and I were newly separated. Our kids were two, five, and eight. It was his night to have the kids, but I just popped by to drop off some unnecessary item I knew they couldn't live without. (The item I was dropping off was actually my fear that they were not okay without me.) But as I entered the one-bedroom apartment I saw my former husband cooking delicious food, with music playing and my kids dancing while they set the table. I was so shocked, I had to sit down on the couch to absorb that they were all surviving without me running the show.

In recovery, one of the best things I did was to make a commitment to myself that Monday nights were all for me. The kids spent Monday nights at their dad's house, so this was my night to say *no* to the rest of the world and *yes* to me and my well-being. No work, no housecleaning, no meetings, no dates, and no going out anywhere. Giving myself this time not only improved my sanity, it also benefitted my kids greatly. I was able to be more present, grounded, and calm to handle all the challenges and blessings of motherhood.

I heard about another woman who found time for herself by hiring a babysitter. When the sitter arrived, she'd walk out the front door and then sneak in the back door and tiptoe up to her room to take a nap.

Sober Mom's Tools to Stop Being Supermom

1. Give yourself a permission slip to say no to the next ten requests for your time and energy. A polite way to say no is, "Thank you so much for asking me, but I have an appointment at that time." Only you have to know that your appointment is your naptime!

2. Take Erma Bombeck's advice: "When my kids become wild and unruly, I use a nice, safe playpen. When they're finished, I climb out."

3. Take a "mommy time-out." If your kids are young, put on a video (even if it's the fifth time they have watched it that day), make sure they'll be safe, then go into your bedroom and lock the door for a brief time.

4. Make a list of everything you think needs to be done today. Then review each item, asking yourself, "Will the world fall apart if I don't do this today?" Now burn that Superwoman cape and post this sign on the refrigerator: *Your emergency is not my urgency.* Here's your new mantra: "I have enough, I do enough, and I am enough." Write it on the bathroom mirror in red lipstick. Post it on the refrigerator. Put it on your dashboard in your car. Stick it to the forehead of your children and spouse and if that doesn't work, get a tattoo.

* * *

11

Anger

The truth will set you free, but first it will piss you off.
— GLORIA STEINEM

Most men can have a heated argument with a buddy and then just let it go. They slap each other on the back and walk away laughing. They seem to have been taught that anger is a natural part of life.

Women, on the other hand, usually receive the opposite message; we learn that being angry (or even honestly expressing genuine emotion) is somehow wrong. Perhaps we have seen women in our family "grin and bear it" while stuffing every injustice deep down inside. Some of us are not taught that our feelings are necessary and valid. So when faced with the pain of frustration at a person or event, we turn our anger inward and blame ourselves for even having the feelings. Those feelings have nowhere to go, so we turn to alcohol or other drugs to soothe them.

We don't have the healthy safety valve for expressing our anger. We don't know how to be assertive without being aggressive. Society often gives women a bad rap. How many times have we heard powerful women in politics or the arts called *demanding* or *bitchy* when they just want to do a good job? Men with these same qualities may be called *decisive* or *strong*.

It's no wonder that after we get sober, all the old frustration and pain eventually rises to the surface. Sometimes this takes us by surprise, as if we are suddenly being hit with a feeling of ancient rage. Our back and neck tighten; we might feel like screaming, hitting something, or crying. This is normal. It comes from all the times we needed and wanted to scream *NO* but stuffed our anger instead.

A huge part of healing in recovery is learning to honestly express our anger in therapy, with a sponsor, or with a skilled professional in group therapy. I attended a family of origin workshop where we did role-playing to deal with anger issues. One of the attendees, Nancy, asked me to play the role of her father. The therapist running the group instructed Nancy to look at me as if I were her father and tell me why she was angry. She began to shake, cry, and yell, "Dad, you spanked me when I was just a little girl. You took my pants down and hit me with a belt over your knee. I was humiliated and felt violated. The worst part was that I had no power—you were bigger and you could beat me as long as you wanted."

Nancy was so spent by this exercise that she finally dropped down to the floor, and we comforted her there. Shortly after, she went into intensive therapy. All the years she had held that pain in—she didn't feel she had anyone to tell, and she was amazed when the therapist told her it was child abuse. Nancy had thought that maybe all children were spanked that way.

Slowly, Nancy began healing from all that suppressed pain, fear, and rage. She took self-defense classes because she wanted to know she could defend herself as an adult. She also took an assertiveness workshop and learned how to firmly but gently ask for what she needs. Nancy is a fearless warrior for her own healing. She learned that we have to teach people how to treat us and that we can firmly say no.

In sobriety we learn to face and accept anger as a human emotion that everyone experiences. By doing the Twelve Steps, especially the inventory steps (Four and Five), we see that what is really underneath the anger is fear—fear we will lose something we have or not get something we desire. When I was angry I felt out of control. I didn't have any tools to process my feelings, and it scared me. When I was afraid to yell and scream I'd go right into hurt and sadness. I expressed my anger by pouting, sulking, and playing the victim. I'd plan my plot to get back at those who had angered me or done me wrong. The Twelve Steps have taught me tools to process my anger, protect myself, and see if I owe someone amends.

I recall many times I was furious with my ex-husband. Early on after our divorce, we couldn't talk in person, on the phone, or email each other without having a huge, knock-down drag-out fight. (Thank God there wasn't any texting back then!) I'd be in the car with my kids yelling at him on the phone. This fighting was no different than the fights we had when we were married, yet the feeling of guilt, shame, and fear of what the divorce was doing to my kids haunted me. I realized one day this fighting had to stop: I had hung up on him in mid-sentence and I'd started telling my kids how horrible he was. My nine-year-old daughter said to me, "Mom, I don't want to hear you talk about Dad this way." My five-year-old son said, "Yeah, Mommy, it's not nice to call people bad names." You know those times when your kids stop you dead in your tracks and the realness of what they say hits you right in your gut? Well, this was one of those moments.

I called my sponsor to tell her about the fight, hoping she'd be able to wave some magic wand to make my anger and guilt go away. I also thought she would agree with me about how awful he was and feel sorry for me. Well, she did not want to hear how awful I thought he was, nor did she seem to feel sorry for me. Instead she told me, "Pause when agitated." Now I was even more agitated, and I was sure she wasn't hearing me right. What's this "pause when agitated" crap? She told me to go read pages 87 and 88 in the Big Book of AA. What's more, she suggested I call my ex-husband to tell him I was sorry for how I behaved and apologize to my kids for yelling at their dad and calling him bad names. I was stunned. But the next day her suggestions were still swimming around in my head and wouldn't leave me alone, so I decided to try her advice. When I called my ex, his voicemail kicked in (thank God!) and I left a quick message saying I was sorry for yelling at him. I also apologized to my children. Even though I wasn't really sorry for yelling at my ex, I did feel better for apologizing to my kids.

That night I had a dream: my former husband and I were standing on opposite sides of a brick wall. I took a brick from the wall, but instead of throwing it at him, I threw it behind me. It was as if I were throwing the brick behind me to get rid of all the anger that was between us. Then my ex took a brick and with all the anger he could muster, he threw it behind him. Brick by brick, we tore down the wall standing between us. By the end of the brick throwing, we were laughing and playing like two little kids. I then woke up to the realization that if we were able to get rid of the anger we were holding toward each other, the two of us might be able to co-parent our three beautiful children in the healthy, loving way they deserved.

If there's a person, place, or thing you're resenting and you can't resolve your feelings around it, I have a suggestion that works every time. Yes, *every* time. If you're at all like me, you're going to hate it. You might not want to do it and you'll likely think I'm insane. But I've seen the biggest miracles happen *every single time* I've taken this suggestion, and each time I think it's not going to work.

Here's the suggestion: simply pray for the person or thing you resent. And here's how I first learned about it: I was bitching and moaning to my sponsor about my ex-husband's new girlfriend. I wasn't interested in getting back together with him, but I was shocked when he found someone new—how could I be replaced so easily? This is where the phrase "laugh out loud" is very appropriate. I expected my sponsor to join me in my bashing session, but instead she suggested that, for the next six weeks, I pray for this woman to have all the success, love, and happiness I wanted for myself. I didn't think she had heard how awful this woman was and how miserable she was making my life. I told my sponsor, "Don't you hear me? I hate that f***ing bitch." She said, "Okay, start with that, because God can handle your anger." Even though I didn't believe it would work, I decided to try it.

So I started each day with this prayer: "Dear God, I pray for the f***ing bitch to have all the love, success, and happiness I want for myself." In about a week I dropped the f-word and continued the prayer with just the b-word. Eventually I was able to say the prayer without any profanity. Today the woman I once hated is married to my former husband. And I can say that she has been a godsend in our life. She has been there so many times for my children and me, and our lives have been so blessed because of her. She and my ex now have two adorable children who I love and who bring me endless joy. We all celebrate Christmas together and I am welcome in their home. My anger was never about her, it was because my ex had a relationship and I didn't.

I love what happens when I suggest this exercise to my clients and sponsees. Most of them look at me with the same disdain I felt toward my sponsor. I had a phone session with a client of mine named Jane. Near the end of our conversation, she spoke of a woman she could not stand. I let her vent for about two minutes and then I stopped her in mid-sentence and suggested the F***ing Bitch Prayer. She said it was the craziest thing she had ever heard but agreed to try it.

One of the best things I love about being a life coach are the messages my clients leave on my voicemail. Most of them begin with, "Rosemary, you'll never believe it!" Yet, I smile with the knowledge that miracles happen all the time when we try to do the right thing and let go of what we are holding on to so tightly. This was true with Jane as well. Jane prayed the prayer every day, and after about a month she and this woman she couldn't stand decided to meet to air their differences. Today they are best friends and she tells me how she would have never been where she is now if this woman hadn't come into her life. They raised their kids together as sober moms supporting each other every step of the way. I could tell you many more stories like this but instead I suggest you try it yourself for six weeks and see what happens.

Sober Mom's Tools for Dealing with Anger

1. If you have deep pain and feel out of control with your anger, find a coach or therapist to work with.

2. Get physical: beat a pillow, turn up the music in your car, roll up the windows, and scream at the top of your lungs. Throw rocks in the water, naming the anger as you throw each stone. Release the anger in ways that do not harm yourself or others.

3. Write out a Fourth Step and work through the Fifth Step with your sponsor.

• • •

12

Sexual Trauma

*It's often said that a traumatic experience early in life
marks a person forever, pulls her out of line, saying,
"Stay there. Don't move."*

— JEFFREY EUGENIDES

Statistics show that one in every three women will be the victim of sexual assault during her lifetime. Women who are alcoholics or addicts are even more likely to have been assaulted or to have experienced some form of sexual trauma. Trauma can be described as a deeply distressing or disturbing experience that may or may not include physical injury. These experiences may be from our childhood—for instance, growing up in an alcoholic home—or they may be from more recent situations or relationships. Either way, the trauma we carry has many faces: physical, mental, emotional, and spiritual. And at some point in our recovery we need to look at these traumatic wounds, because not dealing with them can lead to relapse. The program of recovery serves as a safety net where old pains, hurts, and traumas can come to the surface to be healed.

My sponsee Louise faced a long-suppressed trauma in her early recovery. When she was about ninety days sober, she was having sexual relations with her partner when she suddenly had a visceral reaction in her body. It was so strong that she jumped out of bed and ran out of the room. Louise wanted to scream, as her body was gripped with panic. She had just remembered being molested by a friend of the family during her childhood.

Luckily, she happened to have an appointment with her therapist the next day. While she was embarrassed to bring up the subject of sexual abuse with her male therapist, he could tell that something was bothering her and gently asked her what was happening. Louise felt safe enough to say, "I have this horrible memory that I'm not sure is true." He wisely told her, "We could discuss the traumatic memories in depth, but because you are newly sober and fragile, I would recommend that we just let them surface in their own time."

Louise continued working on her recovery but about five years later was still having flashbacks of the sexual molestation and experiencing other effects. At this point, she went to a female therapist who specialized in trauma work and who used EMDR: eye movement desensitization and reprocessing. This therapy has been used for people who have experienced severe trauma that remains unresolved. EMDR helped Louise process her painful memories and reduce their impact on her life. Her therapist explained that the nature of childhood sexual abuse is such that we doubt that the incident occurred and it starts a vicious cycle of not trusting ourselves at a core level. Part of Louise's healing included changing the way she was parenting her children. She'd been hypervigilant about their safety, and she was overprotecting them and restricting their activities. As a result of the EMDR therapy and working the Twelve Steps in recovery, she was able to appropriately relax her parenting style and her efforts to control her children's safety.

Facing past traumas and doing the work of therapy takes courage. Louise was willing to do anything to release the painful past. Today she is a woman of power, helping others heal from sexual trauma. She is sharing what she learned. As Sharon Salzberg so beautifully put it, "Someone who has experienced trauma has gifts to offer all of us. They have the depth of their knowledge of our universal vulnerability, and experience of the power of compassion."

Another woman I know—let's call her Diane—experienced sexual trauma and then went on to help others find healing. When she was five years sober, a stranger broke into her home and raped her. This was a woman who had created a great life in recovery—she was fully involved in the program and had a host of friends in the fellowship. Diane had been working, going to school, and enjoying her life. But after the rape, she struggled with recurring feelings of shock, fear, and being violated.

On one particularly bad day, she went to the nearby home of her sponsee for support. The next day at an AA meeting the people in the fellowship surrounded her with love and protection. One of her trusted friends in the program offered to come to her house and sit by her bed so she could feel safe enough to sleep. A woman who managed a women's recovery center, and who had also been raped, invited Diane to move into the center for a month. Here, Diane found a safe environment where she was surrounded by other women who understood her pain. It was a godsend. Diane recalls their unconditional love, reminding her that we are never alone, and that no matter what, we don't have to drink or use.

Because Diane had been working the AA program for years, she knew the healing power of identifying with others who have been through the same experience. She next went to a counselor at the university she was attending and asked her to start a women's rape recovery group on campus. Diane knew that to continue healing she would need to be with other women who had been raped or abused. The counselor put a meeting notice in the university newspaper, and women came from out of the woodwork. Some had been raped years ago and never told anyone; others were victims of domestic violence. Women in the group were from every socioeconomic level and walk of life.

The mothers in the group were able to talk about how to pass on the lessons to their children: how secrets keep us sick, and we must find courage to tell someone when we have been abused or traumatized. Healing happens and light comes in as we share our stories. Darkness, fear, and secrets are the enemy. They are defeated when one woman steps forward to speak her truth and light the way.

The group gave relief and healing to all the participants. As we hear in the AA program, "Our experience can benefit others," so we can be there for each other.

As I sat listening to Diane tell her story with such courage, my heart was filled with horror and compassion. She looked at me straight in the eye and confidently said, "Today it's not so much about the event or the tragedy, but about how the program and its people become our rescue."

Sober Mom's Tools
for Healing Sexual Trauma

1. Trauma counseling and therapy: By all means get competent outside help. Interview therapists to find one who works for you. There are residential treatment centers specializing in trauma. Local rape crisis and sexual assault centers can be found in every community. These centers and hotlines offer 24-hour confidential services including counseling

and groups. Some centers will send someone to accompany you to the hospital and be present when the police interview you.

2. Take a self-defense class; if possible, find an age-appropriate class you can attend with your children on this or another subject.

• • •

13

Codependency

A good codependent wakes up and asks her partner,
"What kind of day am I going to have?"
— ANONYMOUS

The core need of a codependent is to mother, manage, fix, or solve problems of those close to us so we can feel in control and safe. We want to micro-manage the world, tell people how to drive, tell complete strangers how to raise their kids, tell our partners what to wear, what to say, and how to even breathe. Symptoms of unhealthy dependence sound like this: *I'm not okay unless everything outside my skin is okay.* Or, *If there are any problems in my children's life, then I can't be okay. If my kid is okay, then I'm okay.*

Once I caught myself cleaning my sixteen-year-old's room, making his bed, folding his clothes, straightening his desk, and gathering his dirty clothes. I realized that I was really just seeking a way to connect with him—and he wasn't even home, so it was a false sense of connection. I had no business doing for him what he could do for himself. It was clear that I was craving connection with him, but cleaning his room was not an intimate conversation. Of course, when I'm doing for him what he needs to do for himself, it leads inevitably to anger. Codependency will place me in a position to be hurt because

I really want credit for everything I do. I want him to appreciate me and think I'm the best mom in the universe. But all he'll think is, *Why did she go through my room? Does she think I'm hiding a girl in the closet?*

We overdo in the mistaken belief that it will make us more valuable. As a codependent, I want my co-workers, lovers, parents, friends, and the world to notice that I'm the best. I think there is no way I'll ever be enough, so I overdo, wanting all my kudos to come from the outside world.

Sometimes the lengths we go to manipulate and control another become humorous. Judy wanted her husband to stop drinking and thought that it was actually in her power to make him stop. She bought a huge whiteboard and a red marker, and set about diagramming her plan for him.

Day 1: Pour out all the liquor in the house and go around town telling the liquor stores to stop selling to him.

Day 2: Tell him he has to stop playing golf so he won't drink in the clubhouse.

Day 3: Suggest that he needs to join a church and get religion.

And so on.

You can imagine what happened. By day four he was actually drinking twice as much and not coming home in order to avoid her! Today, Judy's husband is sober and this story always gets a laugh when he tells it in AA meetings. We learn in the Twelve Step programs that a person has to want to change and we can't make them. They'll just resent us if we do. So we need to take care of ourselves and get out of the way.

One woman I know confided that in the throes of her codependency she had managed her son's education to a ludicrous degree. In high school he started smoking pot and slacking off. His grades took a nosedive so she began doing his assignments for him. She read the books, did the papers, and coached him for exams. She was getting a good education but he sure wasn't, nor was he learning life skills and discipline. He graduated because she had done the work. She next applied to college for him, and wrote all the entrance essays. Meanwhile he was blissfully smoking pot all day. He was accepted and when he started college, she ordered all the books for his courses and did all his work again! When her husband asked why the sudden interest in microbiology and calculus, she lied and said she just thought the subjects were interesting. Her husband also became angry because she stayed up every night to do "her" homework, and she never gave any time to their marriage.

For me, it was easier to take care of others than to actually do what it takes to take care of myself. I learned that when we're in the grips of thinking we know what's right for everyone else but not looking at ourselves, we end up blaming, pointing fingers, and getting resentful because "they" need to change. We may find ourselves thinking or saying, "Why isn't anyone doing anything? Why isn't anyone doing something about this mess? Why can't everyone just do what I say?"

Even after all these years of recovery, I still have these thoughts and lash out at others from time to time. Then I beat myself up and blame myself for reacting this way. Thinking others will change on my time and my watch is futile. I know it's insane to expect the world to get my memo and obey me. I still get caught up in my disease of control, which is based on fear and false reality. But today I catch myself much sooner.

Often, when I have the urge to tell someone to do this or that, I try to stop, look into the mirror, and tell myself to do the same thing. I have to resign from being Queen of the Universe.

Our program of recovery brilliantly tells us that we are no longer running the show. When we let go, we realize there is something much greater in charge, and when we align ourselves with a Higher Power, situations ultimately turn out better than we could have imagined.

The solution to all of my overdoing behavior is to stop and connect to my spirit. This is where I find my internal "enoughness."

For a mom, there is nothing worse than to have her kids hurting. Yet it's the nature of life that there will always be the chance of a bad grade, of not being invited to the "in" party. There will always be the horrible insecurity of the teen years. If we pin our happiness and peace on how our kids are doing, we'll always be upset. Instead we need to find ways to be compassionate, loving, and still detach enough to be able to walk through the day without falling apart.

The solution for me is to take a time-out, just like I used to give my kids when they were misbehaving. When I'm feeling codependent, I take time to step back and see my part in what's going on, take radical self-care such as taking a nap or going for a walk, or spend time with gentle friends who will support me and lead me back to a path of serenity and recovery.

Sober Mom's Tools
for Healing from Codependency

1. Write yourself a "time-out" slip and then list three things you need to do for you instead of others. Then choose one of these ways to put yourself first.

2. Write your "Queen of the Universe" resignation letter. Begin with "I hereby resign from trying to control, fix, or force . . ."

3. Go to an Al-Anon or a CoDA (Co-dependents Anonymous) meeting.

4. Turn the focus back on your life and take your own advice. Whatever it is you want someone else to do, look in the mirror and say out loud what you want that person to do. Now go do it for yourself. For example, if you want your loved one to go to a meeting, go to one yourself.

5. Talk to your kids about what you're learning about codependency, and engage them in developing a healthier relationship with stronger boundaries.

• • •

14

Living the Dream

Never underestimate the power of a dismissed dream.
I think there must be a place inside of us
where dreams go and wait their turn.

— SUE MONK KIDD

As women in recovery we have already done the impossible by getting sober. Now in recovery we have the luxury to follow our heart's desires, knowing there's a good chance our dreams will come true.

The great acting coach Michael Chekhov told his students, "If you want to work on your art, work on your life." Sometimes we need to begin working on our dreams and our creative impulses in order to discover our life. In recovery, our life becomes our work of art.

Sometimes we don't know *how* to do something that our hearts desire, and it's scary. So we do nothing at all. *What if I fail?* we wonder. Well, at one time you didn't know how to be a mom, and the first time you held your newborn baby it was probably a bit scary. But there were nurses and friends to offer guidance. More than likely, you also discovered that you knew more about being a parent than you thought you did.

If you're bored, unsatisfied, frustrated, and sick of your own complaining, then do something about it. Go out and take a class. Join a club. Just do something different. Yes, it may feel odd and scary, but so was being a parent at first. Do it anyhow. Who knows, you may meet a new friend. Have fun, be bold, and remember you've already done the impossible, so the options are limitless. Recovery is full of miracles. The old saying "You can't get there from here," becomes "Well, I *thought* I couldn't get there from here, but I *did* _____ ." (Fill in the blank: learn to ride a horse, write a blog, go back to school.) As noted in the Big Book, "We have found much of heaven, and we have been rocketed into a fourth dimension of existence of which we had not even dreamed" (page 25).

What are some of your dreams?

What have you always wanted to be, see, do, and experience? Write a book, learn to dance, sing, paint . . . ? I spent many years waiting for my dreams to somehow just happen. I was so caught up in the fantasy that I didn't have to actually do anything. It was safe. Doing nothing meant I wouldn't fail. Then I eventually realized doing nothing was worse than failing. The biggest risk is not risking at all. I looked around and everyone seemed to be doing fabulous things with their lives. I was envious: he plays the guitar so well, she's a beautiful dancer, and she runs marathons. I realized it was up to me to design and live the life I really wanted. No one else was responsible for my life but me. I realized my dreams were not going to chase me! The thought of taking action was still scary but I found comfort in this quote by M. Scott Peck, one of my favorite authors:

> The truth is that our finest moments are most likely to occur when we are feeling deeply uncomfortable, unhappy, or unfulfilled. For it is only in such moments, propelled by our discomfort, that we are likely to step

out of our ruts and start searching for different ways or truer answers.

This quote got me thinking about what I wanted the rest of my years to look like and the contributions I wanted to bring to the world before I died.

I was nearing fifty and realized it was time to get busy living while I'm dying. While I still wasn't exactly sure what I wanted to do, in my heart I knew what I wanted my tombstone to say: *She used up every bit of love, compassion, and joy she had, and gave it to others while here on Earth.* I also reflected on how horrible my life would have been if I hadn't gotten sober and encountered all the women who had helped me throughout my recovery journey and my journey as a sober mom. In the Twelve Step rooms, I looked around and saw so many young girls and women needing help and guidance. Many of them would come up to me and ask me to sponsor them, but because of my codependency issues my Al-Anon sponsor suggested I only have three sponsees at a time. Well, I already had four and was frustrated I couldn't sponsor more. I really wanted to pass on the guidance I had received. Then I thought to myself, *The way to help more women would be to write a book.*

Shortly after this realization I went to a women's recovery retreat. One of the exercises was to stand up in front of the crowd and say what you would do if you had no fear. When it was my turn I stood up with shaky knees and burst into tears as I said, "I'd write my books." It was as if my dream of becoming an author had suddenly burst out into the world. There is something very powerful about saying what we want out loud to others. The other side of it is, *Oh shit, now I have to do it.*

At the retreat I was inspired by a woman who had started

taking dance classes at the age of fifty. I asked her how she overcame her fear of starting something new. She said, "I decided I had to be okay with being really bad at something in order to get better at it. Once I started getting better at dancing I decided I had to be okay with being mediocre." At the retreat I read about how author Sue Monk Kidd announced to her husband and kids one day that she was going to be a writer. She refers to that now as her "great absurdity" but also said, "we should all have one or two of those in our lives. A hope so extravagant it seems completely foolish and implausible."

About this same time, I also started watching the talent TV shows *American Idol* and *The X-Factor*. I think I was drawn to these shows because all the contestants were stepping *way out* of their comfort zones. Some were discovered to have amazing talents, others, not so much. But all of these brave people dared to reveal their God-given talent to millions of TV viewers all over the world. I remember Simon Cowell asking one woman why she wanted to be the next American Idol. She told him, "I don't want to die with this music still in me!" Those words struck me like a bolt of lightning. I asked myself, if these people are out there chasing their dreams, then why am I sitting on my butt just wishing I were a writer? (If you've ever heard me sing, you'll be glad I decided to write instead of singing. God gave me the motivation to write; others got the singing thing!)

So I started writing, one sentence at a time, one thought scribbled on a piece of paper. Then I bought a notebook and put it in my purse; anytime I had some great inspiring thought I'd jot it down. Then I bought an iPad and started waking up early in the morning to write. I hired a writing coach and eventually my dream of being an author came alive.

We all have different dreams, but I believe they can all be

achieved if we give ourselves the chance. Ellen, one of my sponsees, kept complaining about her low-paying job and her abusive boss. I asked her what she would do if she could do anything. Ellen said, "I'd really like to be a yoga instructor but I can't because I don't know how, I'd be scared, and I don't have the money for the training." I told her to visualize herself, a year from now, getting certified as a yoga instructor and to even "see" herself teaching a class. She agreed to try and later told me, "The visualization made it real for me. I could see myself teaching and loving it!" I told her to stay with that feeling, to hold on to the dream. Fear flees when we pursue our passion.

She made a plan to go online and research yoga schools and to apply for a job as a counter person at the studio where she was taking yoga classes. She got the job and was soon promoted to manager. "What's next?" I asked her. Ellen said she really wanted to enroll in school to become an instructor, but she didn't think she'd ever be as good as the talented teachers who taught her classes. I reminded her she's already done the impossible by getting sober and suggested she apply despite her fears.

Then one day I got a call from Ellen, and during our conversation she casually mentioned she'd been accepted to the yoga school. I told her it didn't seem like she was too excited about it. She replied, "Well, it doesn't matter because I don't have the money to go anyhow." I reminded her that she was in charge of the footwork and God was in charge of the miracles. I believe that if you tell God the *what,* God will show you the *how.* Well, the *how* showed up for Ellen with the $10,000 she needed for the yoga program. The program was six days a week, twelve hours a day for seven straight weeks. She had to travel eight hours from home and live in a hotel with another student she'd never met.

Ellen started the course, but one day she called me completely exhausted and overwhelmed, saying she didn't think she could continue. I reminded her she only needed to do one hour at a time and suggested she go to bed and decide tomorrow whether to leave. It was the same principle that helps us stay away from alcohol or drugs. Sometimes we need to focus on one hour at a time, and when all else fails we go to bed and tell ourselves we can drink or use in the morning.

Ellen woke up the next morning and decided to continue with the training. She came home and started teaching yoga classes and I again asked her, "What's next?" She said "I'd love to go to New Zealand or Australia and teach yoga for three months." I suggested she go online and look for jobs. She found a position, applied, and a few weeks later left me a voicemail saying, "Rosemary, you'll never believe it! I got the job in Australia teaching yoga for three months in a studio."

After returning from an amazing three months in Australia, guess what I asked her? You're right, "What's next?" Ellen said, "I'd love to open a yoga studio." In the past year she has gotten married and recently became pregnant. I've decided not to ask, "What's next?" for a while, as she's going to have her hands full soon, but I'm looking forward to when she opens her new studio someday. Most of all, I'm looking forward to witnessing another sober mother holding her new baby and the miracles that continue to happen when we put down the drink and the drugs.

What dreams do you have locked up in you that are waiting to be expressed in the world? What is God or your Higher Power trying to express through you? I don't care who you are or where you come from, there are many talents planted within you. Go find yours! Sit quietly to hear the longings of your soul. Do not die with the music still in you!

Sober Mom's Tools
for Making Your Dreams Come True

1. Ask five people in your life, "Where do you see me limiting myself?" and "What do you think I'd be good at?'

2. Ask yourself, *What would I do if I had no fear?* and *What would I do if I knew I could not fail?* Write down your answers on a piece of paper. Tell three supportive friends about your dreams. Keep journaling. Take baby steps toward realizing your dreams—and then pursue another dream.

3. Hire a coach to keep you accountable or find an accountability partner and support each other in fulfilling your dreams.

4. Pray to God or your Higher Power: At times I think you forgot to plant in me gifts and talents to bring into this world. Remove those thoughts and show me what my talents are. Help me to step out in faith, one baby step at a time. Lead me to those people who would help guide me to find and use these talents. I know these talents are all expressions of love from you to the world. I thank you for these special talents and gifts. I will do my best to use these gifts you gave me. My gift to you is to try to use up every ounce of talent you have given me before I die to enhance another's life.

• • •

15

Joy and Laughter

I love people who make me laugh. I honestly think it's the thing I like most, to laugh. It cures a multitude of ills.

— AUDREY HEPBURN

You're sick and tired of being sick and tired, you have no more fight and no more answers, and you feel beaten by alcohol and drugs. You walk into your first Twelve Step meeting probably dreading what you will find: a bunch of sourpusses who are having no fun (ever again) and who are pissed off (because their "medicine" has been taken away). Instead, someone is telling a horror story about being drunk and stupid, and everyone laughs. How shocking—aren't these people supposed to be super serious? Now you almost feel angry with them for laughing and feeling good, because you are hurting so bad.

Next you notice the laughter and joy are contagious, that everyone is finding humor in some event that would shock and horrify "normal" people outside the meeting. All of a sudden a woman describes an event while drinking that sounds suspiciously like your own experiences and you're laughing right along with them.

So many of us say that our first Twelve Step meeting was where we laughed for the first time in years. The levity can be such that we think we've walked into the wrong room. The humor in the program is the best kind: it's "Me, too!" laughter. *Yes, me, too. I did that also. I felt that way. You are like me and we are not alone.*

Steve Allen said, "Comedy is tragedy plus time." Nowhere is that more true than in recovery. We did certain things while drinking that were so embarrassing we swore we would never tell a soul as long as we lived. Yet, miraculously, our stories become funny when we are clean and sober. An old-timer gave me this prayer, "Lord, teach me how to laugh, but never let me forget how I cried."

One hysterical story I heard was from a woman who shared about her Club Med vacation, in a tropical paradise, while drinking. Enjoying the free cocktails in the bar, she got liquored up, picked up a man, and agreed to move the party to his room. On the way, she spontaneously jumped into the pool, fully clothed. This was a habit, pool jumping; she'd also climb trees while drunk and get stuck in them. Of course she was in a blackout during the pool incident. When she woke up to daylight and blinding-hangover hell, the man was not in the room. She also discovered she was naked and her clothes were nowhere to be found. Oh my! She finally peeked out the sliding glass door and saw that her date had apparently hung her clothes on a lawn chair to dry. So here she was naked in the room and her clothes were *outside*. Now that is a problem most non-addicts don't run into. The room was right off the pool and at this time of day there were people everywhere. The classic drinking dilemma: waking up naked and not being able to get your clothes! As she told her story in that AA room, everyone was laughing along with her because they could relate. I once heard a guy joke, "You may be an alcoholic if you find yourself coming to on a Greyhound bus, naked."

Laugher truly is the best medicine and it's the shortest distance between two people, because when we laugh with someone we are bonded. She who laughs, lasts! Look around the rooms; you'll see that the healthy people are frequent laughers and there is a light, a twinkle in the eye. It's said that children laugh 164 times a day and the average adult laughs about seven. Of course, we all know people who seem to have had their sense of humor surgically removed.

This is one of the gifts of being a mom in recovery. Our children can teach us so much about letting go, laughing, and being joyful in the moment. Let's face it, after we are grown it's the silly, ridiculous things we did as children that become the favorite family stories. Tell your kids funny stories about your childhood. We can let our children show us the humor in life, and we can show them, too. At dinner tell your children a funny story about your day and ask what was the funniest thing that happened in their day.

Both laughter and its spiritual sister, joy, have a common way of surprising us. When we hear a funny line, it's usually funny because it's unexpected. The same way we are surprised by laughter, we are surprised by joy. A friend of mine has a plaque in her bathroom that reads *Joy is the infallible sign of the presence of God.* Indeed, moments of pure joy, from deep within, spring up and catch us off guard. Often it's a feeling of everything being right with the world, that we are just as we are supposed to be.

For me, joy feels like my insides are giggling. As with love, you can't buy joy. Yet joy is all around us in the simple things in life. I find joy in watching my children laugh together. I have experienced the thrill that joy sends through my body when I watch my children play sports. Each year around Christmas time I decorate a gingerbread house with my daughter and my former husband's two young children. I see the excitement this tradition brings to their sweet little faces and I feel joy. When I go to AA chip meetings and watch people walk up the long aisle to receive their anniversary coin and celebrate their time in sobriety while everyone applauds, I feel joy fill the room. The more joy you give to others, the more you will know joy. And when you are present, you'll be able to notice all the joy surrounding you.

When I am stressed out and over-*doing,* I seem blinded and shut off to joy and laughter that is always available to me if I am connected to my *being.* At these times, I try to take a break and unplug from the world and my to-do list so I can get back to just being. Once I took myself on a trip to the coast for two days to recharge—no phone, computer, TV, books, or journals. As I headed north up the California coastline, I could feel my shoulders relaxing. The beauty of the trees, sky, mountains, and ocean calmed my soul. As I continued to soak up these amazing surroundings, I felt a kidlike joy deep inside me. I decided to play with that joy. I pictured myself literally stirring it like I was stirring a huge pot of decadent melted chocolate. The joy grew bigger and bigger. This was the first time I had done this—just really basked in joy. I also realized how often I have done the opposite and focused on trouble and problems. I can take a bad feeling, comment, or situation—you name the yuck—and can go deep into that pot of crap and stir away, making it bigger and bigger. When this happens, I can feel it in my body until it seems to boil over and consume me. It's true what good old Abe Lincoln said: "Most people are just about as happy as they make up their mind to be."

While I was away for those two days I started looking for joy. It was easy to find. I felt joy as the sun sparkled on the ocean. I smelled it in the wonderful aroma of the sea that reminded me of summers spent at the beach with my family growing up.

I heard birds chirping and singing the most beautiful tunes. I watched two playful and carefree birds as they engaged in what seemed to be a game of tag. I sensed a place inside me where joy lived and the voice said, *Come out and play.* I understood in that moment that joy is God's gift to us, and She wants us to play and enjoy this beautiful life we've been given.

We've all felt the depths of pain when we were in the thick of our addiction. Joy eluded us as we chased the blissful high. Following is a passage I wrote when I was in deep pain but I hung on to the AA slogan, "Don't quit before the miracle." I knew the journey through the depths of my depression would somehow lead to joy:

> The journey from pain to joy is not a straight one. It twists and turns. It can feel like an exhausting climb up a steep mountain. There will be deserts, windstorms, dark nights, and times when you will collapse from complete fear. There will be long moments of loneliness and despair. Tears may pour down so heavy but at the same time you will meet many blessings along the way. Strangers will become your new best friends and bring you laughter and moments of joy. When you seem to be lost, guides will suddenly appear and point you in the right direction. You will reach vistas and see views so beautiful it will touch your soul deeply. You will feel the up-close presence of a Higher Power that will heal all that pain just by standing still and breathing Its presence. The sun will shine so bright and warm your heart as it beams far into the distance so others will be drawn to you for warmth and comfort in their darkest days. You will be their guide along their way. As you walk with them and share your experience, strength, and hope you will find yourself at the top of

that mountain that once seemed unreachable. You will find a new strength deep inside yourself and a life beyond your wildest dreams. The person will turn to you and thank you and you will realize that the pain took you to a land of joy and miracles you could have never imagined. My wish and prayer for you is this: Let pain be the gift of healing into joy. When we face pain, suffering, and heartbreak, we are offered a journey to an unknown land of healing, connection, joy, and gifts beyond our wildest dreams.

Sober Mom's Tools
for Experiencing More Laughter and Joy

1. Do something for the kid in you every day. Play in the rain, stomp in the puddles, make sand or snow angels, have a water fight. Ask your kids to join you.

2. Laugh at yourself; don't take yourself too seriously.

3. Go to a comedy show or watch a funny movie.

4. Play games. Some of my favorites are Twister, Cards Against Humanity, Loaded Questions, and a family favorite—charades.

• • •

16

Spirituality

God often speaks to me through Christian Dior.

— GIGI STOPPER

Spirituality is a big part of the Twelve Step program. Many who are new to the program struggle with this at first because of bad experiences they've had with religion. Some only have to hear the word *God* in the rooms and they go running out the door. But the spirituality that the Twelve Steps speak of isn't about religion. I once heard someone describe the difference this way: "Religion is for people who are afraid to go to hell, and spirituality is for people who have already been there."

In recovery, spirituality means many different things to different people. And that's the beauty of the Twelve Step program—it encourages us to find a Higher Power of our own understanding. People use many different words to describe spirituality or their Higher Power. I say use whatever word suits you. Here are some words I hear in the fellowship when people are talking about their Higher Power: the Source, Higher Self, Buddha, Jesus, Higher Love, Lord, Force, the Divine, Mother Earth, Great Warrior, and Spirit Guide. I even heard one person say she used the word *doorknob* for her Higher Power because she wanted her doorknob to open doors for her that she couldn't open herself. Who knows, someday we might come across a bumper sticker that reads *Doorknob Is My Co-Pilot,* or see people wearing doorknobs on a necklace chain or setting up statues of doorknobs in their garden!

Many women new to the program have a problem with the idea of a male-centered God or Higher Power. Indeed, it can be hard to see yourself as powerful when *power* has a male face. We find that in most cultures the images of God are strictly male. Most religious literature uses the male pronoun, and so does the Big Book of Alcoholics Anonymous. Is it any wonder, then, that some women make men their Higher Power? As Mary Daly put it, "As long as God is male, males are God." This seems like another injustice, because women have suffered such abuse and suppression at the hands of men. If a woman was abused by her father, partner, or other male figures, the last thing she'll want to do is "turn her life and her will over" to another man once she finds recovery.

But even though the world we live is in still predominately male-centered—and men hold much of the political, religious, and financial power—in recovery, we get to choose our own concept for God. We are free to ask, why does God have to be a He—why not a She? Or why do we need to use the term *God* at all? As we continue working the Steps, some of us long for—and choose—a feminine spirituality, a feminine face of God.

Sometimes in Twelve Step meetings, when reading the Big Book, a woman will replace the word *He* with *She.* (The Big Book of AA was published in 1939, and at that time, most of the people in the early groups were men, and the language reflects that.) Some will go ahead and identify a Higher Power that is female. Jan, who was raised Jewish, says she was relieved when her sponsor told her she could create her own concept of a Higher Power. Since Jan is in show business, she chose a sort of Mae West goddess concept. She wanted her goddess to be fun-loving, full-figured, butt-kicking, and boa-wearing.

Before I walked into the rooms of AA for the first time, I felt like an empty shell. My spirit was dead. At about ninety days sober, when the alcoholic fog started to lift, I read in the Big Book that "Our sobriety is contingent upon our spiritual condition," and I thought, *Oh shit, I'd better get to work on this spiritual thing or I'm screwed.*

Yet I confused spirituality with religion at first, and religion had always been a struggle for me. I grew up Catholic, a religion with many rules, and I had broken them all. I had a skewed concept of God. On the one hand, I heard about a loving God; on the other, I learned that He/She/It would throw me into the flaming pit of a hell if I said a bad word. It never made any sense to me. It also seemed very odd to me, even as a young child, that Catholics were the only people we believed were going to heaven. And it certainly didn't seem fair that only men got to say the Mass. I thought, no thank you; this religion thing did not appeal to me in the least.

Then when I walked into AA, I heard about finding a "God of our own understanding" and turning our will over to this God. Somehow I believed God's will for me would not be what I would have chosen. I was afraid God would decide I should become a nun and my life would consist of dreadful poverty and chastity. I had visions of living like the nuns I had encountered as a child when my father took us to daily mass during Lent. We went to a small chapel where the Carmelite nuns lived. These nuns took the vow of silence—the only time they could speak was when they were praying, which they did while hidden behind a screen. As a kid, I was always afraid I'd be sent to live with these nuns if I misbehaved. Now, as an adult new to recovery, the thought of not being able to drink or speak—well, I couldn't imagine anything worse!

When I told my sponsor how I struggled with the "God thing," trying to figure who and what God was, she asked me what I would want if I could design a God of my own understanding. My list went something like this: warm, loving, a guide to show me a beautiful life, funny, and compassionate. She said, "Great! There's your new God. Go seek this God and let me know what happens."

In my search, I went to churches, prayed, read books on spirituality, went on retreats, and talked to spiritual teachers. I was almost like a child on a treasure hunt, looking everywhere for buried treasure. Bottom line, I was always searching outside myself to find God. But I felt most comfortable with what I heard in the rooms of Alcoholics Anonymous. I loved hearing people talk about the miracles they experienced in the program. I saw with my very own eyes people walking into the rooms who were battered, sick, broken, and with their lives in shambles, and then I'd see miraculous changes and healing start happening. I figured only a power greater than any human could turn these people around. And I knew that AA provided this healing help to anyone who was willing. I felt the presence of a Higher Power in the rooms of AA and the people there were kind, loving, and compassionate. Many people use AA as a God of their understanding; some say God is an acronym for "group of drunks." Once I heard "You don't have to understand God—apparently God understands you because She created an entire program for and about you."

At six years sober, I was mired in a dark, deep depression. This had lasted for about six months and I couldn't snap out of it. People were telling me, "Go to more meetings, do the Steps again, and get another sponsee." A therapist told me to take more naps; a psychiatrist told me to eat more carrots and celery. Nothing worked, and the depression was getting worse. I had no idea why.

Then one day I felt out of hope, and the only options I saw were to drink or die. I knew I really didn't want to do either of these, plus I had three children who needed me. I finally decided to check myself into a local treatment center. I just needed a safe place to go so I wouldn't drink or hurt myself.

I had been there about a week and it was my birthday. I remember sitting on the lawn thinking, "What the hell am I doing here, stone cold sober for six years, at a treatment center with a bunch of newly sober people? Did I make a mistake coming here? Please, God, if I am supposed to be here, give me a sign— and a cake, flowers, and a gift would be nice too." I yelled at God, "What the hell are you thinking, God, and where are you?" As I sat sulking that day, I had a stirring feeling in the pit of my stomach and for the first time in my recovery I felt the presence of God within me. By this point, I'd been searching outside myself for years, trying to find God, never knowing God's presence was also inside me.

Since that day I have never doubted God's presence with me. In her book *Firstlight,* Sue Monk Kidd talks about her inner life. For her, finding the reality of her inner life was like "cracking open a raw longing for the Divine and exposing an irrepressible hunger for that deepest thing in myself." She described exactly what I felt that day. It was as if I'd reconnected with a long lost friend or reunited with a former lover. I also realized the hole I had once tried to fill with alcohol was the very place inside my spirit where my Higher Power resided. Instead of filling that hole, the alcohol was drowning out my connection to my Higher Power.

That night, I got the birthday gift I'd asked for. God sent a sign I could not miss. On Wednesday nights at this treatment center, alums come in to share their stories. I was blown away when the speaker walked in: she was the same woman who'd told me when I was ninety days sober that she'd just returned from the treatment center for her depression. To see her that night was my miracle. All the stars were aligning. As chills radiated through me, I knew I was right where I was supposed to be. That was my best birthday gift.

From that day forward I have always known two things for sure: the presence of God is within me and in our darkest moments, gifts will arrive when we least expect them. Chuck Chamberlain, a beloved AA speaker, used to say, "God hid himself in the last place we'd ever look—inside ourselves."

During my search for God, I discovered that most religions were teaching the same ideas that humans crave: community, peace, love, guidance, and an understanding of something much greater than ourselves to help make some sense out of this crazy world in which we live. To me a Higher Power is beyond human understanding. What I found buried sometimes in the darkest places were beautiful gifts that I never knew existed.

If you are struggling with your concept of spirituality, you might ask yourself where or when do you feel your spirit come alive. For some, Spirit comes alive when they are sitting by the ocean, walking among trees, hiking in the mountains, or listening to music. I often can see my Higher Power in the eyes of babies and dogs. For me, when a baby is looking at me I hear Spirit saying, "Hi, there, Rosemary; it's me, God." I look back and say, "Hi, God, I'm glad you are watching over me."

While I have never received a phone call, text message, or email from God, I have heard Her talk to me in other ways. One time I was taking a walk along the beach in Santa Monica and talking to God. I remember wanting an answer on some earth-shattering problem that I was struggling with. There I was, standing at a stoplight about to cross the street, when I heard God loud and clear: "Wait, the stoplight is on. Wait, the stoplight is on." I know God works in mysterious ways, but never did I expect Him to speak to me via a stoplight. The answer to my question was to wait, and that is exactly what I needed to hear.

Another time I was anxious about finding a job. I had been doing a lot of footwork and wasn't having any luck. On this day I was cranky and upset, feeling as if God had forgotten about me. I was online trying to get into my bank account and my computer was taking its sweet time to load. I kept hitting buttons on the keyboard, hoping to speed things up. Now I was mad at God, the bank, and my computer. A message flashed on my screen: *Please be patient while we process your request.* I laughed out loud and got it. The computer had restored my faith. God hadn't forgotten me after all. My job was to be patient, keep doing the footwork, and leave the results to my Higher Power. Within a few weeks I received a call from a company that had done some restructuring and they wanted to hire me for my dream job—it had not existed two weeks prior. I sometimes picture God playing a giant chess game, moving the pieces around on the game board of my life, repositioning obstacles in the way, reminding me to play and have fun.

When they start working the Twelve Steps, some of my sponsees say they don't believe in a God or Higher Power. Some are atheists or agnostic; others have been harmed by religion. Some are like me; they grew up attending church but never experienced a close relationship with God. I let them know their beliefs or non-beliefs are perfectly okay, and I ask them to just work through the Twelve Steps and see what happens. I tell them the Twelfth Step promises we will have a spiritual awakening as a result of doing the Steps. And, if you ask me, there is something *very* spiritual about the Twelve Step program and the Steps—that an addict who has tried everything to stop drinking or using and then, by working the Steps, "suddenly" is not picking up that drink or drug anymore. Regardless of how my sponsees start out, they all come to believe in a "power greater than themselves" and their lives change for the better.

I found that one of the most difficult places to practice the spiritual principles in all my affairs was at home. The principle I had the most practice with was in Step Ten: "Continued to take personal inventory and when we were wrong promptly admitted it." My kids heard me apologize and make amends again and again: "I am sorry and I need to make amends." I also tried to use this same strategy to help my kids when they were fighting. I'd separate them and tell them to go think about their part in starting the fight. Then, when they were calm, I would have them tell me what they were going to do to try and change their behavior. One day I realized my daughter had actually been paying attention when she came home and told me she had "made amends" to a girl at school who she had been mean to. I thought, *Hallelujah!*

I didn't really want to stop drinking the first day I entered AA, but I did want to feel some peace. I had forgotten what peace felt like. Today I know for certain that I feel peaceful when I can offer peace to another human being. A feeling of calm washes over me. When I came into AA, my spirit was dead, but the people in AA loved me until I could love myself. The highest form of spirituality, I believe, comes from offering love and compassion to another, and from being a mirror to help others see the amazing beauty that exists inside of them. This is what AA did for me. To me, this is spirituality, this is a Higher Power working in my life.

My journey in recovery has been to continue to discover

the light inside me so I can shine a light for others along their path. I wish I could tell you what gifts are waiting for you, but these gifts are different for everyone. Whether you are one day sober or a double digit-er, the gifts are there. All you have to do is stay sober, one day at a time, and the gifts will continue to appear.

Sober Mom's Tools
for Discovering Your Spirit

1. Write a personal ad for your Higher Power; list the qualities and powers you desire your God to have.

2. Do things that nourish your soul: walk in nature, play with babies, or do an act of kindness for someone else.

3. Search out ways to meditate, listen to a guided meditation, say a simple prayer, and talk to your Higher Power as you would a friend. Pour out your heart and feel the presence.

. . .

17

Communication

You can talk with someone for years, every day,
and still, it won't mean as much as what you can have
when you sit in front of someone, not saying a word,
yet you feel that person with your heart,
you feel like you have known the person forever . . .
connections are made with the heart, not the tongue.

— JOYBELL C.

Some of our most basic human desires are to be seen, heard, and understood. This is the basis of communication—to see and hear another and have them see and hear us. As moms in recovery, it is so important to give this gift to our children, to take the time to really listen to them, giving them the feeling of being heard.

The Twelve Step program is a place where we can develop and hone our communication skills. Let's face it: many of us didn't grow up with role models who exhibited the best interpersonal skills. Before recovery, my communication skills were slim to none. When I wanted to talk about a problem with someone, it always became a heated argument. I would yell or scream so the other person would see I was right and come over to the winning side. (My side, that is!) I often gave people the silent treatment, which I later learned was a form of manipulation.

When I was with friends, the topic of every conversation was usually "Poor me, ain't it awful?" or "Can you believe what he did?" I'd endlessly tell anyone who would listen how terrible my situation was and why the person I was angry with was 100 percent to blame. And all the while I was talking to people who couldn't do anything about my problems in the first place. I had so many arguments in my head with people who weren't even in the room. I might as well have let them crawl into bed with me, because they were in my head keeping me up all night anyhow.

While I was married, discussions frequently turned into verbal fights and nothing got resolved. Afterward, I felt so uncomfortable about the altercation that I would over-apologize. Going from anger straight into guilt, I'd put all the blame on myself. Sure, we are supposed to accept and make amends for what we have done, but taking all the blame is self-destructive behavior. When it comes to taking responsibility, we are to "clean up our side of the street." Because of my guilt (sometimes *old* feelings of guilt), I'd try to clean up the whole neighborhood!

As a result of working the Twelve Steps, I've learned how to talk to people directly. And it's been a long time since I've had interactions like I used to. Now when I react poorly, I use the Ninth Step and make amends as quickly as I can. I have learned that, in most situations, none of us is right or wrong; we just have different perspectives. I've learned how to pause, get clear about what triggered my anger (not pointing fingers), and see my part. This allows me to walk away as a dignified, sober woman—and that feels good.

In recovery, I've also found the value of something simple in communicating: Listen to the other person! Now when I need to express my feelings about something that is bothering me, I use this formula: I approach the person calmly and say,

"I'd like to talk about the situation. Are you available to meet sometime?" To just say, "We need to talk" is controlling and self-seeking, as the person might not be ready to talk yet. Or she may choose to never talk, which is her prerogative. If she says yes, then I use these steps:

1. I say how important the relationship is to me.

2. I explain what upset me and how it made me feel. ("I felt hurt and insignificant to you when we planned to spend time together and you were an hour late and didn't call.")

3. I state what happens for me when I feel this way ("When I feel hurt and insignificant I want to run away and say screw you.")

4. I restate how important the relationship is to me and ask for what I'd like. ("When this happened I felt I wasn't important to you. Our relationship is very important to me and I don't want to push you away. It would be helpful to me if you're running late to give me a quick call.")

This same formula works well for resolving problems with our children. Just being present for our children is a huge gift. When your children are upset the best thing you can do for them is to sit down and give them your absolute, undivided attention. Sometimes we aren't always available right in the moment, yet we can say, "You seem really angry, and I want to hear about it. Can we talk about it when I get home?" Remember we all need to be seen and heard to feel valuable. Ask your son to tell you what is going on or ask your daughter why she is upset. Don't interrupt. Just let your child talk. We know how uncomfortable it is to be filled with feelings and have nowhere to go with them. So we give our children the gift of letting them release their feelings in a healthy way. This also gives the message that we do not expect them to be perfect, and it's okay to have these feelings. Doing this also goes far toward enhancing your child's self-esteem, which comes from being accepted for who they are and for feeling whatever they feel. Remember, feelings are not "right" or "wrong." They just are.

My favorite story about communication—or rather, miscommunication—is the "soccer bag" story. My ex-husband called one morning to tell me he was running late to get the kids to school and himself to work, but our daughter had forgotten her soccer bag at my house, and she needed it for afterschool practice. He asked me to leave it by the front door, and he'd swing by to pick it up. As I rushed out the door to work, I put the soccer bag right by the front door as I said I would. Ten minutes later, he called me, furious, saying, "Why didn't you put the soccer bag by the front door?" I spit back, "I did put it there." We fought back and forth: "No you didn't," "Yes I did," "No you didn't," "*Yes I did!*" At some point we figured out we were both right—the bag was right by the door. But he thought I meant outside the door, and I thought he would know I meant inside the door. Oh, if we could have just read each other's minds, it would have been so much easier. I actually remember saying once in couple's therapy how I just expected my husband to know how I was feeling. Poor guy, I assumed he'd bought the special glasses that could read my feelings.

Another communication skill I learned in recovery was about anger and not taking things personally. When I encountered someone who was angry, I was advised to picture that person as a hurt small child who wanted someone to listen and validate his or her feelings. How would I respond to such a hurting child?

Here's an example of how I was able to change my reactions based on this image and other new skills I was learning: My ex-husband called me one day, really angry with me. I took a deep breath, knowing that other people's anger is about their fear, so I tried not to be defensive. I just said, "Wow, you seem very angry at me." He then proceeded to give me a few reasons why he was angry. I responded, "I can understand how you could feel this way. (Remembering that feelings aren't right or wrong.) Is there anything else you're angry with me about?" He paused for a long moment and I'm guessing he looked down at the phone to see if he had dialed the right number as he wondered, "Where did my crazy ex-wife go?" I then clarified what I had heard and asked, "Did I hear what you are saying correctly?" He paused again and said, "Yes." I then asked if he was willing to hear what I had to say. He agreed and I calmly told him my view. We discussed the issue. The old me would have tried to get him to see my side and how I was *right,* or I would have given in and said he was right and I was wrong. Back then, I didn't know that people could disagree and just leave it at that. After we'd both voiced our opinions, I ended the call by saying, "Well, I've said everything I need to say. And unless you have anything else to say, it looks like we differ on this issue." When I hung up the phone, I realized it was the first time I was able to really listen to him, say what I needed to say, and respect both of us as individuals.

A client named Amanda was upset at her husband because their wedding anniversary was coming up and he hadn't made any plans for them to celebrate. I asked if she had talked to him about what she'd like to do. She said yes, that she kept telling him, "We need to talk about making plans right now." I pointed out to her that saying "*We* need to talk about this now" is a boundary violation and controlling behavior. If *you* need to talk to someone about something, that doesn't mean the other person is required to have the conversation. A more respectful request is, "I'd like to discuss xyz. Are you willing and able to have this conversation?" People do have choices, and they may not always make the choice you'd like them to make. Some of the choices are *No; Yes, but not right now;* and *Yes, and let's talk now.* Learn to accept all the answers equally, not just the ones you want to hear.

Remember, our children are watching how we communicate and interact with others. It's our job as mothers to model healthy behaviors for them.

Sober Mom's Tools for Better Communication

1. When discussing a problem with someone, try the formula used above: "When _____ *(state what you are upset about),* I felt _____. *(name a feeling—hurt, sad, disregarded).* When I feel this way I want to _____ *(describe the way you really want to react—i.e., scream, run away, give the silent treatment).* What I would really like is for you to _____. Do you think you are able to _____?"

2. Take a "time-out" when you are really angry—especially with your kids. Make sure you tell the other person you will resume the conversation after you have cooled down. If things can't be solved, remember it's okay to agree to disagree.

3. Try to understand the other person's point of view and stay on your side of the street!

4. Read the book *The Four Agreements* by Don Miguel Ruiz.

• • •

18

Worry

Stinkin' thinkin' leads to drinkin'.

— AA SLOGAN

In an AA meeting, I once heard a speaker say he wakes up in the morning and there's a vulture on the bedpost. Before he is even fully awake the vulture says, "Oh, I'm glad you're awake. I need to tell you a few things. You aren't good enough, you fall short, others are skinnier, richer, and smarter than you."

We really need to shoot the vulture! The vulture is our stinkin' thinkin'—that negative voice that keeps us stuck in self-doubt and worry. Worrying is like being in a rocking chair. You go back and forth but you don't really get anywhere. Most of us moms in recovery are black-belt worriers. As a matter of fact, we probably think that if we stopped worrying the Earth would surely stop spinning. We feel it is our duty call to mind every scary thing that might happen to our children, our home, the planet, and us. When in a state of worry, we are so hypervigilant that it can drive everyone around us crazy. The very best thing that we can do for ourselves and our children is to stop fear-based worrying. Worry is absolutely contagious, and the twins Negative Nancy and Nervous Nellie are no fun to be around. Get away from them as soon as possible before you turn into Worry Wanda.

A friend of mine says she caught the worry bug from her grandmother and mother. They were always afraid the other shoe would drop; they never imagined it might be a glass slipper. I find it interesting how we don't get caught imagining happy endings. My friend said that one day when she was two years sober her roommate came home and found her sitting on the sofa in an agitated state. The roommate said, "Hey, what's the matter, did you get some bad news?" She replied, "Nothing's the matter—that's why I'm worried." We have to laugh about our nutty thinking.

Worry doesn't help anything, action does. When we come into recovery, one of the first things we learn is to take life one day at a time. Some days the best we can do is one moment at a time, because only in the present moment do we have nothing to worry about. In recovery our sponsors will tell us stinkin' thinkin' leads to drinkin'. This includes worry, that circular, repetitive, addictive thought process that goes around and around in our head.

At eleven years sober, I finally understood I had a "thinking problem." I had worked the Steps many times. I was active in AA and Al-Anon. I went to meetings, had a sponsor, and many sponsees. I had a career I loved, three amazing kids, great friends, and a wonderful extended family. I was smart, successful, and decent looking. I felt good about myself and knew I had a lot going for me. But I was still plagued by negative thinking: *You're not enough. You will lose your job and you will die a lonely old lady with cats crawling all over you.* I know I'm not alone with these negative thoughts. Most of us are walking around expecting of the worst. Not enough money, not enough time, not smart enough, and not pretty or skinny enough. It was time for me to finally do something about my negative thinking and I said to myself, *Enough of this "not enough" stuff!*

I heard the greatest stop-worrying remedy. A woman was telling her sponsor about her laundry list of fears, "What if I lose my job? What if my child fails her grade? What if an asteroid hits my house?" The sponsor pointed out that the woman was future-tripping and finally said, "Look, we can't shovel the snow until it snows. When it snows, I'll come right over with a shovel, but let me remind you, we live in the desert." This little story helps me so much when I start to get into obsessive, circular thinking. As Mark Twain said, "The worst things that ever happened to me never happened."

Our greatest worries as mothers are about our children. The very best thing we can do for them is to demonstrate how to take action instead of worrying about something. We can't be effective today if we live in a state of worry. If we have one foot in the future and one foot in the past, we're missing the present.

One of the best tools I discovered was the God Box. You can make one yourself—a shoebox will do, with or without a slot and a label on it. When I was worrying or obsessing about something, I'd write that thought on a slip of paper and put it in the God Box. For me, the physical action helped me let it go. Sometimes I put the same worry in day after day. One day I thought, *Well, if my Higher Power can take care of all the bad stuff, why not put some good stuff in the box?* So I started putting in my hopes and dreams, such as going to Hawaii, becoming an author, meeting a wonderful life partner, putting money in the bank, and making a new friend. From time to time, it was fun to go back and reread what I had put in the box. The worries all seemed to work out just fine, and what seemed so catastrophic in the past was sometimes humorous months later.

In these simple ways we can give our children tools that will serve them for the rest of their lives. What a gift! When my children came to me with a problem, I would listen and often end the conversation by suggesting, "Say a prayer and let it go. Let God surprise you."

I had to learn that myself when, after my divorce, my kids were no longer with me every night. Split custody meant that they were at their dad's house half of the time. One night, my youngest child Joseph called from his dad's. He said, "Mommy, I need you. Come get me." My husband would not let me come over to pick Joseph up. He said, "You can't rescue the kids every time they want you." It was heartbreaking, but it was the new reality. I comforted my son on the phone until he was okay. My heart was breaking for my child, and I wanted to just hold him tight. I was in bed doubled over in pain, crying my eyes out. Then I visualized all my children being held by God, in a warm blanket being rocked to sleep. I asked my Higher Power to wrap me in the same warm blanket and rock me to sleep.

Fast-forward fifteen years, and that same boy called me yesterday. He'd been waiting months to hear from the college rugby coach whether he'd been chosen for early acceptance to attend and play for his first-choice college. I talked to him, using all the tools I learned in recovery: "Honey, you've done everything you can, so now try to let go and trust that you will go to the perfect school for you. It sounds like you're making up a story about what you think might happen. Since you don't really know yet, you might as well make up a good story. Say a prayer, and I know it's all going to work out just like it should." Two hours later he called back with the news that the coach had personally called him and told him he's on the list.

My son James caught the worry bug, and he was fixated on my safety. When he was at his dad's house he'd call me and ask, "Mom, did you lock the doors and make sure the stove is off?" He was worried I couldn't take care of myself, and he wanted to protect me. When he was a teenager I was always asking him,

"Did you do this? Did you do that? Don't forget x, y, and z." Once, when we were driving in the car and I was into my worry routine, he said, "Mom, you always worry, and it stresses me out!" I said to him, "You're right. I need to stop worrying. Let's make a deal. I won't worry about you, and you won't worry about me." There was a sense of relief and we were able to enjoy the rest of our day together.

Recently, James and I were again driving in the car when he asked me if I was dating anyone. I said, "No. Why do you ask?" He said, "Well, Joseph's leaving for college soon and I'm just afraid you'll be all alone." I told him I would never be all alone, and he said, "Oh that's right! You have AA."

I heard a woman in Al-Anon say that she always worried about her kids, and her living amends was to not worry about them. In recovery we need to stay aware of our thinking or we run the risk of relapse.

Sober Mom's Tools for Letting Go of Worry

1. Tell your stinkin' thinkin' to go away and replace the negative thought with a positive thought.

2. When you're worrying, ask yourself, "Is there an action I can take right now about this situation?" If so, then do that instead of worrying.

3. Surround yourself with positive people.

4. Try meditation. It's a great way to quiet the mind.

5. Get or make a God Box. Put all your worries, hopes, and dreams in it and see what happens.

• • •

19

Surviving Domestic Abuse
and Violence

I'm not crazy or unstable—I was abused. I am a survivor.

— ANONYMOUS

We might think of domestic abuse as something dramatic we see on an episode of *Cops:* the 911 calls, the bandaged woman, and the man being dragged to jail. These are the type of stories that make the headlines on the ten o'clock news. Yet abuse occurs behind closed doors of the quiet house on the block as well. And, like addiction, domestic abuse is no respecter of a person's status. Its victims include women and men; those who reside in mansions, are well educated, and lack for nothing as well as those in unsafe neighborhoods who aren't sure where they will get their next meal. The common denominator is that these people live in fear of more abuse. They feel shame because they know they need to leave, but they feel trapped.

Children are casualties of this horror as well. Imagine how terrifying it must be to see your mother being abused and knowing you are powerless to stop it. The scars from witnessing violence in the home can carry over into generations. Children who grow up in an abusive home are more likely to be victims themselves or to become abusers.

Not all abuse is violent and ends with a 911 call. Much more insidious and prevalent is the emotional abuse that gradually eats away a person's confidence. We can lose our very self when we are continually manipulated and told we have no value. Sexual abuse occurs when there is coercion to do something against our will or we are treated in a sexually demeaning manner. This definition from the Department of Justice website describes the scope of abusive behavior:

> Domestic violence is a pattern of abusive behavior in any relationship that is used by one partner to gain or maintain power and control over another. It can be physical, sexual, emotional, economic, or psychological actions or threats of actions that influence another person. This includes any behaviors that intimidate, manipulate, humiliate, isolate, frighten, terrorize, coerce, threaten, blame, hurt, injure, or wound someone.

I met Latoya when she had a couple years of sobriety and was getting help for the long-term effects of domestic violence. In describing her relationship, Latoya said she was flattered and felt loved at first when John, a charming man, wanted to be with her all the time, and she was happy that he liked to drink as much as she did. It was a three-way affair that included Latoya, John, and booze. Although she loved having his undivided attention in the beginning, soon it became claustrophobic. Months into the relationship, he questioned why she was late coming home from work. He was irrationally jealous and accused her of being attracted to the men at her workplace. Latoya thought John's behavior was a result of his troubled past and decided to give him yet more love and attention.

As her partner became more possessive of her time, she just gave in and stopped seeing her family or girlfriends. Latoya's life became isolated. Then John began using hard drugs, and everything got worse. He'd rage at her and beat her up, then the next day repent, bringing her flowers, begging for forgiveness and tearfully promising to never do it again. The make-ups were as intensely passionate as the fights were violent.

John was a master manipulator and able to twist reality, convincing Latoya the fights were somehow her fault. "If you didn't nag me, I wouldn't lose my temper; you're the problem," he'd insist. Since she'd been in a haze or blackout, she was easy to influence. And she took the blame.

After one horrible, frightening night when John had her down on the floor beating her, she vowed to herself that she wouldn't take it anymore. She called a crisis hotline and went to a shelter. Finally she was safe, and she learned through listening to other women's stories that she was not alone. The counselor firmly told her, "You are not at fault; you just need to heal." A little while into her stay in this safe environment, Latoya admitted to her counselor that her drinking was out of control. The counselor took her to some women's AA meetings, and here she found a community of women who'd had similar experiences with alcohol. The program of AA, along with therapy, helped Latoya reconstruct her life. She regained some of her power and inner strength, and her life started to change.

At first, it was hard for Latoya to look at the old patterns of her life. She had difficulty not re-creating the same destructive relationships from her past, but with help from her recovery friends, today Latoya knows that she is worthy and that her life is important.

Another woman, Lee, says the first time in her entire life she felt loved by someone unconditionally was when she started working with her AA sponsor. Her sponsor only wanted what was best for her and wanted nothing in return. Previously, all her intimate relationships had been full of pain.

Lee met her future husband, Xavier, when she was in college. Xavier was dynamic, and a successful businessman who made her laugh. He was very sweet and good to Lee at first. But the longer they were together the more Xavier criticized and intimidated her. First it was about her cooking: "This dish tastes like crap—can't you learn to cook? Do I have to come home to this?" Next it was the way Lee dressed: "You dress like a hick; you have no style. I'm ashamed to be seen with you." She started to feel like nothing she did was good enough and so she tried harder, while sinking into despair. Undermining a person's self-worth or esteem is abusive and one of the most destructive human behaviors. Constant criticism can rot away people's core feelings about themselves.

Unfortunately, this kind of attack was not new to Lee, as she had been the family scapegoat growing up. Her two sisters had been put on a pedestal and held up as perfect little darlings while Lee had been the target of her parent's rage, frustrations, and unresolved issues. Along with the verbal abuse, she was slapped, backhanded, and hit. "You just aren't right. I wish I never had you. You're stupid and you'll never amount to anything," she was told again and again. She internalized these thoughts and insults. She says, "I believed what my parents said about me as a child, that I was no good. Later, it felt natural that a man would tell me the same. My reasoning was, 'Well, if you think that about me it must be true.' I had grown up with a litany of abusive insults from the time I was a little girl. So life with another abuser was familiar." It is said that we go to what we know. Women who have been abused and intimidated are likely to unconsciously be attracted to another abuser.

Xavier was good at keeping her dependent by controlling the couple's money. And, knowing that her drinking was out of control, Lee felt guilty and sometimes thought she deserved the bad treatment. Over time, Xavier started making fun of Lee in front of their friends, using sarcasm to hurt her. Xavier was taking his own feelings of anger and rage and directing it sideways on to Lee, just as her parents had done. When they were both drunk, the abuse escalated, the fights got more vicious, and a few times he hit her. Mostly the abuse was more insidious, constant, erosive, and manipulative. *If you don't do what I ask, I'm going to make your life hell* was the message.

She says, "If I'd been strong enough I would have immediately run in the other direction when he started to treat me this way. In sobriety I learned that the chains that bind us are too strong to break by the time we realize they are there." At the time, she wanted to save face and work it out, because this was her second marriage and she was too ashamed to admit she'd made yet another mistake. Drinking helped block out the reality of this miserable existence.

Like a lot of abusers, Xavier threatened that he'd get custody of their son if Lee left. "Any judge would give me custody because you're a lush." Threats are a major way abusers keep their partners in a state of fear. Lee told me she feared daily that she'd better do what he said or he would take her child away, leave her friendless and destitute.

Lee's turning point finally came when she saw in living color what the abuse was doing to their six-year-old son. The family was boarding a plane and Lee started to take the window seat. Xavier ordered her to sit on the aisle. He yelled in front of everyone, "Bitch, sit where I tell you." Her six-year-old son repeated what his father said: "Yeah, bitch, sit down." It was a shock to see her young son patterning his father's behavior. Lee then realized this scene also mirrored her parents' treatment of her.

The end of the marriage was particularly cruel. Lee was in the hospital recovering from cancer surgery. Xavier came in and announced that he was leaving for Europe with his mistress, and he was serving Lee divorce papers. That's what drove Lee into her first Twelve Step meeting. For months she cried through every meeting. But recovery saved her and gave her back her life.

Since she entered recovery, Lee has gone back to school and earned a doctorate degree. She is now a professor at a top university, a star in her field, and published in scholarly journals. The road she traveled to get to where her life is today is one of those miraculous journeys we hear in the rooms of AA and other Twelve Step programs. She endured abuse in her childhood and marriage that could have completely destroyed her if she had not gotten sober. Through working the Steps in recovery, she acquired many tools and developed a stronger sense of self-worth. As she describes it, "I'm much more centered and grounded, less vulnerable, and have a healthy dependence on my Higher Power. God has done for me what I could not do for myself. I'm proud of my academic and professional achievements and through this work I'm able to help countless other women. When temped to go down the rabbit hole of crippling self-doubt, I call my sponsor and go to an AA or Al-Anon meeting. I've come to know that self-doubt and self-hatred are two of the most destructive defects and that I can't afford to stay there. Today I have boundaries. I am compassionate towards my parents but I no longer let them abuse me." Her sense of humor has also returned to the point where she can joke about her ex-husband and use an old Southern expression, "I wouldn't pee down his throat if his guts were on fire."

Although Lee's son continued to imitate the verbal abuse of his father for a time, through family counseling he has since turned around his behavior and now treats his mother with respect. The destructive cycle has been broken, and one woman's sobriety changed everything.

Sober Mom's Tools
for Surviving Domestic Abuse

1. First, know that abuse is not your fault and you are not alone. Get support! There are local crisis hotlines that can direct you to counselors and shelters.

2. If you are still in the home, put together a "safety suitcase." Include a change of clothes for you and your children, some cash, your Social Security card and other identification, so you can leave immediately in an emergency.

3. Ask trusted friends and relatives to check on you.

4. If you are being abused, manipulated, threatened, or feel unsafe, don't be quiet—tell someone. Go stay with a safe family member or friend. You don't have to live this way any longer.

• • •

20

Shame

Shame is the lie someone told you about yourself.

— ANAÏS NIN

Guilt relates to our behaviors and shame relates to who we are and how we feel about ourselves. Guilt is the feeling that *I did something bad,* and this can sometimes point to a behavior we want to change. Shame, on the other hand, serves absolutely no purpose other than to tear us down, chew us up, and spit us out, saying we are worthless. In our worst shame state we find no reason to live. Brené Brown, author of *The Gifts of Imperfection,* says, "Shame is the intensely painful feeling or experience of believing that we are flawed and therefore unworthy of love and belonging." Shame is not based on facts. Shame is the lie we believed when someone told us we were less than, and it's our job in recovery to restore the beautiful, authentic person we really are. In recovery we stop believing the lies.

As mothers, we don't want people to know how inadequate we feel. Often, we bear the horrible shame of abandoning our children to go drink and use, or leaving them with unsafe people. We may have stolen money from their piggy banks to pay for our booze or drugs. We probably lied again and again. Then there are all of the promises we never kept: "I'm so sorry, honey, I was sick. I promise I'll be at your next ballet recital." I've heard women in the depths of despair say things like "I hate my kids and they hate me."

Lisa, a friend of mine in AA, told me her story of shame. She grew up as the second child in a family of five children. Throughout her childhood, her older brother constantly told her she was fat, stupid, and ugly. When she ran to her parents crying with her hurt feelings, they would only tell her to stop crying and go to her room if she wanted to cry. She needed her parents to protect her, to tell her brother to stop being verbally abusive, and to say that he was wrong—that she was beautiful, smart, and lovable. But these needs went unmet, and her brother continued to call her names and insult her. Since her parents allowed this to continue, she figured that her brother must be right and that her parents agreed with him. She internalized these messages and carried them with her all her life. She only had to look around her to find proof that the messages were true. In school, there were students who earned better grades, so she continued to think she was stupid. In the mirror, she saw someone who was fat and ugly. Although she wasn't overweight, she started dieting in fifth grade, but no matter what she weighed, she thought she was fat. And she never felt she was pretty enough for a boy to like her. When she picked up her first drink, she finally found a way to escape the negative feelings that consumed her. Soon, alcoholism preyed on these feelings.

The cycle of shame keeps us from seeing our self-worth and easily leads us back into using and drinking. We dare not tell anyone how we feel and we push down our negative feelings about ourselves. These are the secret shames that can lead us to relapse. For alcoholics and addicts, shame can actually kill.

Maria, a mother of three young children, was struggling

in recovery and kept relapsing. Her shame told her to keep the drinking bouts a secret. She wanted to appear "together" and in control of her life, so she refused to come clean about the relapses. When she did attend an AA meeting she lied and told everyone she was fine. The shame she couldn't stand to feel was for the way she was hurting her children and family by relapsing. She wouldn't talk about her shame when she was sober, but when she was drunk the words slurred out of her mouth: "I wish I'd never had these children. They'd be better off if I were dead. I've ruined their lives. I am such a loser." When she sobered up, she would shower, get dressed and go on with her day. I tried to help her numerous times when she relapsed—once I took her to the hospital and a detox center twice in the same week— but afterward, she never mentioned a word about her four-day drinking binges. I'd ask her how she was feeling and she would say, "Oh I'm fine," and act as if nothing had happened. I realized it was just too hard for her to talk and ask for help because her pain was so colossal and devastating. Unfortunately, her shame and untreated alcoholism eventually took her life and left her children motherless.

Another woman, Cheri, relapsed very briefly on pain medication after twenty-five years of sobriety. Because she worked the Twelve Steps and sponsored other women, she'd had a firm foundation in the program. Cheri was sitting in her regular women's AA meeting when she was overcome with the feeling that if she didn't own up to her relapse, she would fall back into the grips of her disease and never recover again. For her, freedom was telling the truth. She knew she'd be lost if she did not tell her group. Not only was she met with care and love from the group of AA women, but she won even more respect for talking about the dangers of relapse.

At the same meeting a week later, a woman named Lani opened up about her relapse two weeks prior. She said being at the meeting where Cheri admitted her relapse gave her the strength to admit to her relapse as well. Cheri demonstrated that the way out of shame is honesty and courage. We will never know, but perhaps Cheri saved Lani's life by carrying the message that there is nothing to be ashamed of. We have a disease that is treatable when we share it with another addict who understands. When we're controlled by shame it's impossible to feel good about ourselves. Shame is like a giant tsunami that overtakes us with the overwhelming feeling, that "I am so embarrassed to be me."

Jasmine had a mother who suffered from depression. Her mother continually compared herself to other mothers and felt a deep sense of failure even though she was kind and loving. One day, Jasmine's mother told her that she was thinking of killing herself. Jasmine talked her out of it, but she was left with her own irrational shame, thinking if she were a better daughter her mother wouldn't be so depressed.

As women, we seem to easily take on the legacy of someone else's shame. Today, Jasmine is in recovery and has compassion for her mother, but beyond that, she lives in the knowledge that she is free and doesn't have to be a carrier of shame. Recovery is definitely the antidote for shame.

When we come into recovery, one of the most important things we learn is that we have a disease. Addiction is a disease like diabetes or cancer. I once heard in a meeting, "We are not bad people trying to get good we are sick people trying to get well." I had been telling myself that I was the worst of the worst, calling myself names, beating myself up for continually letting my children and family down.

Another woman described her shame, which started in

early childhood: "For my entire life I felt unworthy, that I did not belong. I felt incredible shame when I was just a little girl, terrified that I'd be punished and the punishment of shame is relentless. I was not guilty of anything, it was just a pervasive feeling of doom, fear, and self-doubt."

So many women have this deep sense of shame and when we come into the program we don't just have low self-esteem, we have no self-esteem. My sponsor helped me see that what I really am is an innocent child of a Higher Power. When I started to beat myself up I would say to myself, "God, let me see myself as you see me."

The Big Book tells us in chapter 5, "We ask Him to remove our fear and direct our attention to what He would have us be." These words tell me to imagine what God would have me be. And in chapter 9: "We are sure God wants us to be happy, joyous, and free." I'm certainly not free when I'm indulging in self-hatred. I've come to see that shame, self-doubt, and self-hatred are at the bottom of all my difficulties in life. Someone said, "The only real sin is self-hatred." So what I have learned to do is to say prayers and then return myself to my natural innocent state, which is happy, joyous, and free.

Brené Brown suggests that when we find we are beating ourselves up we stop and say, "Oh, I'm feeling vulnerable." These emotional hot flashes of shame are really just us feeling vulnerable. Most of us have tried to push down vulnerable thoughts at all costs. Yet in sobriety we find that we can feel vulnerable. Now I can sit with those feelings and even gain strength in knowing that I don't have to know it all, be it all or do it all. In the past, I didn't want to have one moment of insecurity or vulnerability so I would cut myself off from relationships, opportunities, and my dreams. Today I can change the way I'm feeling, and the quickest way to do that is to affirm, "I am a perfect version of myself." Or, as Oscar Wilde put it, "Be yourself. Everyone else is already taken."

Self-doubt is born of shame. I used to doubt everything I thought and did. I would second-guess myself, never trusting my intuition. I was sure I was going to fail because I was "not enough" in the first place. Once we have realized the shame we have been carrying around for so long is not our true self, we can move on to find out who we really are. Our true self tells the shame state to go away and stop lying to us. True self says, "I am lovable, capable, and brilliant." True self says, "You are perfect just the way you are and I will never abandon you." True self takes us by the hand, tells the shame state to f*** off and leads us to the amazing things we were sent to Earth to contribute to the world.

When we step out of our shame state and into our true, innocent, and even brilliant selves, we begin to do the things that we thought we could not do. We find that, one small step at a time, we are proving wrong our negative beliefs about ourselves. Today, I'm happy to prove myself wrong by doing things I never thought I was capable of.

Sober Mom's Tools for Overcoming Shame

1. Talk about it: The only thing that heals the feeling of shame is to talk about it with a safe, compassionate, non-judgmental woman who once felt the same way, and who loves us anyway. We need to hear, over and over, that we are worthy, lovable, and talented.

2. Visualize taking the shame out of yourself and handing it to your Higher Power.

3. When your shame comes up, treat it as if you were approaching a young child. Ask this child what she needs and find a

way to give it to her. Most often she wants you to take care of her, tell her she's lovable, beautiful, and safe.

4. When a negative thought surfaces, replace it with a positive one. Your mind cannot hold two thoughts at the same time.

• • •

21

Self-Care

When a woman becomes her own best friend, life is easier.

— DIANE VON FURSTENBERG

Being a sober mom is my greatest blessing, and it can also be my most challenging endeavor. I have a job, and I do all the cooking, cleaning, homework, carpooling, and so on. In all my years of motherhood, not once did I hear my children say, "Hey, mom, why don't you sit down and relax? Let me bring you a cup of tea!" Nor did Mary Poppins or Alice from *The Brady Bunch* ever appear at the door to help out. You may relate.

Before I entered recovery, a typical day for me looked like this: I'd wake up at six, jump in the shower and be dressed by six thirty. Then I'd wake up the kids for school, feed them breakfast, make their lunches, dress my two-year-old, help my five-year-old tie his shoes, and help my eight-year-old with her hair. Next it would be time to rush all of them into the car and drive them to their separate schools and daycare. Then I'd go to work. I was in sales, so I pounded the pavement drumming up business, as I needed to be the number one sales person. By mid-afternoon I'd realize I hadn't eaten all day; I'd only had coffee. Now hungry and tired, I'd stop at the nearest Starbucks and have more coffee and a muffin. After work I'd pick up the kids from school and deliver them to all their sports activities. At home I'd pour myself a huge glass of wine, make dinner, help with homework, have another generous glass, and hurry the kids to bed. When they were finally asleep I'd finish my sales reports along with the rest of the bottle. Then I'd collapse into bed, wake up the next morning, and do it all over again.

During this time, I kept having dreams of a small girl who was alone at the park sleeping on the playground next to the slide. She appeared to be homeless. Her hair was matted, face and hands were filthy, and her clothes were ragged. In my dream a woman would appear to take care of the little girl. At first the woman just sat with her in the sand. The girl was exhausted and needed to sleep. Then the small girl picked up her head slightly to peer up at the woman. Eventually the woman took her home and gave her a bath, washed her hair, dressed her in clean clothes, and fed her some hot food. The woman was kind, compassionate, and caring. The little girl needed someone to hold and care for her. Eventually she wanted to go have fun at the park and play with all the other kids.

Once I became sober, this dream represented who I was and what I encountered when I stumbled into the rooms of AA, ragged, exhausted, alone, and scared. The women in the rooms taught me how to care for myself with a simple formula known by the acronym HALT. If I was hungry, angry, lonely, or tired, I was to halt and take care of myself. Previously, I ran myself so ragged I never stopped to know if my basic needs were being met.

A bottle of wine used to work to relax me and help me escape from the stress, but in sobriety I had to find substitutes for the wine. Bubble baths became my refuge at the end of the day. Sometimes the day seemed so unbearable that I took what I call a "double bubble day": two baths in one day. When my kids started fighting I no longer gave *them* a time-out. Instead I began giving *myself* permission to take a break.

As I continued in recovery, I accumulated a list of other self-soothing remedies that still work for me today. I make myself a cup of hot tea; curl up with my favorite fur blanket and my hot lavender neck roll. I might take a nap, read a good book, walk in nature, call a friend to ask for help, or go see a funny movie. In addition to developing healthy stress relievers, I learned to find creative releases. At first I had no idea what I could even do creatively but I asked myself what I had liked to do as a child. I remembered enjoying painting, dancing, and writing, so I started with those activities. Other than the paint supplies, none of these creative outlets cost me any money.

All of this self-care was vital to my sanity and helped me be a mother who was present and loving towards my children. However, there were days when I was so distraught and exhausted that I literally had no energy to do any of this. I would then call another sober mom and she would give me a simple suggestion for self-care along with permission to take care of myself. Occasionally, I'd have a day when I was pulling my hair out cursing at my Higher Power and screaming, "Hey, I could use a little help down here!" More than a few times there were those miracles where someone who was a good listener would show up at my door or call and offer to take my kids for a while. Those were the days when I was sure there was a Higher Power looking over me! When I found myself cursing at God or the kids it usually meant I needed to learn what self-care really meant.

Physically, I first needed to learn to nourish my body with healthy food, which meant sitting down to eat real food for breakfast, lunch, and dinner. Chowing down a granola bar and a cup of coffee in my car while driving between client meetings did not constitute a meal. I learned the brain needs protein, vegetables, fruits, and a lot of water. Exercise had always been part of my life, and I knew it helped relieve stress. But if I took a day off from exercise from time to time, I could give myself a break and not beat myself up. The twenty-minute nap became a lifesaver for me. Three o'clock was always a low energy time in my day. In recovery, I learned to replace that extra cup of coffee and sugar bomb with a twenty-minute power nap. I would set my alarm for twenty minutes and just rest. Today I am still the queen of power naps. (Thank you, Mom, for teaching me the benefits of napping!)

Learning to take care of myself better did not happen overnight. It took me about five years in sobriety before I could allow myself to take a day off from work if I was sick, or go to the dentist and doctor for regular check-ups. The last, but not least, step in my self-care journey was to finally clean out my closet and throw away my bar drinking clothes that didn't match who I was in recovery.

For my mental self-care, I was taught early on in recovery to journal. Today, I use my journal regularly to vent my anger, feel my feelings, write about my dreams, draw pictures, and clear all the noise in my head. Actually this book is a compilation of many different journals! I finally started reading books again. At times I have three books going at a time. I'd like to tell you I read huge novels like *War and Peace,* but at least in early recovery, I gobbled up every recovery, self-help, fix-me-quick book I could get my hands on. I had a bookshelf full of these titles in my room. (One of my girlfriends suggested I might want to hide these books and journals if I ever planned to have a man up there!) In these ways and more, over the years I have learned to slow down, turn off the phone, computer, television, and radio to enjoy the silence and just do nothing.

Meeting with my sponsor, going to women's meetings, doing a lot of therapy over the years, and crying my eyes out helped take care of my emotional side. I was always told, "Oh, Rosemary, you're so emotional," and I interpreted being emotional as a bad thing. I think what they meant was that I didn't need to kick and scream to express my emotions. I have learned over the years to embrace my emotional side yet to not let my emotions overwhelm me. I started noticing people, places, and things where I felt my spirit light up and stayed aware of where I felt my spirit was being squashed. I then chose to be around positive people who were moving forward in their lives. I went dancing, saw funny movies, went hiking with friends, went driving up the coast while playing games with my children and learning to be my own cheerleader. I stayed away from negative people and walked away from friends who relapsed and didn't want help. As I once heard someone say, "If you hang out in a barbershop long enough, you're probably going to get your hair cut." Since I didn't hang out in barbershops I changed the saying to, "If I hang out in the donut shop long enough, I'm probably going to eat a donut." I also practiced letting people know when my feelings were hurt instead of lying and pretending otherwise.

I learned to rejuvenate my spirit and replenish my soul, unplug from the world and get quiet. I prayed a lot throughout the day, took time for reflection, and finally enjoyed meditation. I noticed the grace of my Higher Power working in my life in ways I couldn't explain. I have learned to accept the unknown and trust in a power greater than myself. I understand now that following my will is easy at first but gets harder as I go. God's will for me is hard to accept at first but gets easier as I go, which really means I can choose short-term gain for long-term pain or short-term pain for long-term gain. I now am awed by the sounds of the waves, the breeze blowing through the trees, birds soaring in the air and feeling the power of God in the majestic mountains surrounding the place I live.

Relationally, I scheduled individual time with each of my children, and I met with friends to have fun and laugh together. I made a conscious effort to visit my parents and siblings, who all lived eight hours away. I called my parents at least once a week and made sure I ended each conversation with "I love you." I stepped out and made new friends. The real stretch for me was to ask for help and allow others to do things for me.

Professionally I have always overworked. Changing that habit was a real challenge for me when I entered recovery, and it still is to this day. In the past, I'd go all out and then crash and take a few days off. When I started practicing self-care, I took all my vacation days and was surprised to discover the company could survive without me! (Just kidding.) I also learned to negotiate pay raises and realized the value I brought to my job. Because I started listening to my inner self, I took giant leaps of faith in my career. I decided to leave a secure job and go back to school to do what I love.

On the financial side of things, I've learned that it's not important how many times you fall down. What matters is how many times you get back up. Well, my knees are often bloody and yet my hands are quite a bit stronger from pushing myself up after each fall. I have grown in the areas of tracking my expenses and understanding where my money goes, reading contracts before signing them, and showing up for my children and myself by going to work. When I am in right relationship with my money and not overspending, I can donate to causes I believe in. My dad always said, "Pay yourself first." Lucky for Macy's I didn't take my dad's advice for a while, and unfortunately my savings account suffered. My father also gave some solid financial advice: save some, spend some, and give some away. I am great at spending some and giving some away; however, I need to get better at saving some. God is my employer and I have always had a roof over my head, gas in my car, and food in the refrigerator. I have much to be grateful for.

Overall I have learned that radical self-care means treating myself with the utmost respect, compassion, and love in all areas of my life. Most important, I learned I am a work in progress, and I thank God for the recovery slogan "Progress, not perfection." When I am practicing self-care I am in a much better position to take care of my children and be a good, healthy role model for them.

Sober Mom's Tools for Self-care

1. Make a list of five things that rejuvenate your spirit. Choose one of those things and do it twice a week. Continue doing this until it becomes a habit and a part of your regular routine.

2. Map out your "radical self-care" day. This emergency plan will be a lifesaver when you feel completely depleted and don't know what to do. For example, here is my plan.

   - Physically: I eat three small healthy meals full of veggies and protein and two small snacks like nuts or fruit. I drink a lot of water and hot tea. I take a walk. I wear clothes that feel comfortable. I take a nap.
   - Mentally: I read and learn something new. I think positive thoughts.
   - Emotionally: I practice staying calm and centered. I relax and take it easy.
   - Spiritually: I meditate for ten minutes and listen to my intuition.
   - Relationally: I spend time or call someone I care about.

- Professionally: I take a day off and shut down my computer and cell phone.
- Financially: I stay within my spending plan.

3. Write yourself a promise letter on taking care of yourself and post it where you can read it daily. Here's a letter I wrote to myself.

I promise to put my relationship with God first.

I promise to be more concerned about disappointing myself than disappointing others.

I promise to care for my physical health by exercising and eating well.

I promise to always speak kindly to myself.

I promise to pursue my dreams and make them a reality.

I promise to love and forgive myself no matter what.

I promise to go easy on myself.

I promise to hang out only with people who light my light, who honor and respect me.

I promise to have fun and laugh *every* day.

• • •

22

Having Fun and Celebrating Life in Sobriety

Find ecstasy in life; the mere sense of living is joy enough.

— EMILY DICKINSON

Having fun and celebrating is something I've always loved to do. The early days of my drinking were lots of fun. I was a party girl, and my friends called me Wild Rose. Back in high school my girlfriends and I started our nights of fun with a bottle of ninety-nine cent Tickle Pink wine apiece—we called ourselves the Tickle Pink ladies! Our favorite thing to do was to grab a bottle, put on our roller skates and skate down the boardwalk by the beach. We would drink, laugh, fall down, and get back up.

One of my first drunks was at my friend Tina's sixteenth birthday party. Her mom had planned a surprise party for her, and my job was to bring her to the party after everyone had arrived. She and I hung out, finished our usual bottle of Tickle Pink, and then went to the party at the prearranged time. Tina was surprised to find about seventy-five high-school kids had gathered to celebrate her birthday. Everyone was having a great time until the moment came for Tina to blow out the sixteen candles on her huge birthday cake. After we all sang happy birthday, my friend Rob and I started a cake fight. Long story short, the party ended when her mother noticed blue frosting all over her brand-new white carpet and started screaming for all of us to get out of her house. That night, my "just having fun" quickly went to having fun with consequences. Unfortunately the carpet suffered more severe consequences than I did.

I continued drinking for the next twenty years, even after I became a mom, until the fun stopped and all I was left with was consequences. When I first came into the rooms of AA, I thought my life was over, that I had been sentenced to a life of lack and limitation. I feared that, without drinking, I would have no personality at all and would become like a hole in the donut—just a dull, boring woman. After all, everything I'd done for years was centered around getting drunk. For me, fun had to include alcohol.

I mistakenly thought my past activities were fun only because alcohol was involved. For example, I loved to dance but I couldn't imagine going to a party and dancing without drinking. I connected dancing with going out to classy bars and dive bars, where I'd be the one dancing on the table. I also loved hanging out with my girlfriends, but our get-togethers always included drinking. What would we do for fun if we had to stay sober? Travel was another favorite activity, but I couldn't imagine flying on a plane without having a few drinks at the bar before or sitting by the pool and not drinking a margarita. How was I ever going to have fun or enjoy life without alcohol? Although I didn't know much about how this AA thing worked, I did know that the goal was to avoid any drinking at all costs and so my former activities were out of the question. What's a girl to do?

Luckily, I told an old-timer in the program about my fear of never having fun again and was pointed to a passage from chapter nine in the Big Book: "But we aren't a glum lot. . . . We absolutely insist on enjoying life." That was a revelation to me.

It continued, "So we think cheerfulness and laughter make for usefulness. . . . Everybody knows that those in bad health, and those who seldom play, do not laugh much." And soon enough, I began to notice that people in recovery were laughing and having fun doing all the same things I used to do minus the alcohol.

My sponsor asked me, "What do you like to do? What do you enjoy?" Like many a newcomer, I had no idea what I liked. She suggested I get active in the program and hang out with the sober people who were living life to the fullest. So I just started doing my life. When I stopped drinking I quickly found out who my real friends were—they were the ones who supported me in my sobriety. My former friends who only wanted the old Rosemary fell by the wayside. Now my friends and I would get together and go for coffee and walks. Soon I met other women in AA and they started inviting me to AA parties. The first one I went to had a deejay, and all these sober people were dancing. Someone told me it used to take her about three drinks to feel comfortable enough to dance, yet in sobriety all it took for her to feel comfortable was dancing three songs. She also let me in on a secret: no one was watching me dance because they were all too concerned that everyone was watching them.

For about five years, a group of us "sober sisters" spent most of our free time together. We threw some of the greatest parties, including luaus, pool parties, birthday, and sobriety parties. We celebrated holidays together and took classes together. We planned elegant dinners, played games, and went snow skiing, water skiing, and camping. We ran triathlons and marathons and played in sober softball leagues. We went to ball games, movies, and concerts. We traveled to Hawaii on vacation and attended sober conventions all over the world. We got our kids together and had slumber parties and picnics at the beach. We laughed, shared meals, and drank *a lot* of coffee. Best of all, we modeled for our children that life can be a lot of fun without drugs and alcohol. Before I knew it, I was having more fun sober than I ever had while drinking and the bonus was that I remembered it! Today, I realize that I certainly did not become a hole in the donut. Instead I've become the fancy donut with sprinkles on top!

By staying in recovery one day at a time, that "fourth dimension" becomes available to us. My own experience mirrored that of Bill W., as he explained it in the Big Book (page 8): "I was soon to be catapulted into what I like to call the fourth dimension of existence. I was to know happiness, peace, and usefulness, in a way of life that is incredibly more wonderful as time passes."

Sober Mom's Tools
for Having Fun and Celebrating Life

1. Find sober sisters who have similar interests, and do things together. When you see another woman in your group who you'd like to get to know, ask her to go for a walk or go to coffee.

2. Get out of your comfort zone and try different activities and hobbies. Start paying attention to what intrigues you and do it, even if it feels uncomfortable at first.

3. Throw a theme party. Include your kids in the planning process and invite their friends or your sober sisters' kids as well.

4. Wake up each morning and be grateful to breathe another sober breath. Find a way to celebrate being sober.

• • •

23

Relapse and Triggers

Don't look where you fell but where you got up.
— ANONYMOUS

The return of an illness after a period of improvement: that's how the *Merriam-Webster Dictionary* defines relapse. We can apply this definition to our addiction, which the medical field agrees is a disease. Unfortunately, when some hear the word *relapse* in relation to drinking or using, they associate it with failure and judgment. People with addiction do not get the same compassion as those with other life-threatening illnesses such as cancer, diabetes, and heart disease. When a friend or family member has another heart attack or cancer returns, the phone rings with sympathetic calls, and casseroles and flowers are dropped off at the house. People ask what they can do to help. No one blames, shames, or judges this group of people. When addicts are faced with "the return of the illness," however, their disease is viewed in a different light. The addict is often shamed or ostracized, and certainly no one's bringing casseroles to the door.

If you do relapse, realize that this is part of your journey and is not a moral failure. You can start over, and you can jump-start into a stronger recovery. It's also a great opportunity to learn what your triggers are and how to keep them from tripping you up again. Yes, there are triggers that can lead to relapse, and once we know what our danger signs are, we can watch out for them. So when we identify the triggers, we can see them as highway signs that say *Danger Ahead* with flashing red lights. The next signs can say *Slow Down* and *Call Your Sponsor* and *Go to a Meeting.*

Many contributing factors can lead to relapse. Here are some of the ones we hear over and over in Twelve Step meetings: holding on to resentments *(I'll show them; I'll drink at them),* staying away from meetings, not working the Twelve Steps, and refusing to ask for help. All of these are addressed in the Twelve Step programs. The formula for staying clean and sober is simple but not always easy to follow.

We can place all of the blame for a relapse on people, places, and things. But let's get real. Our use was never tied to one set of circumstances: We drank when it was raining, and we drank when the sun was shining. We used on good days, and we used on bad days. We drank when we had money, and we drank when we were broke. The bottom line is, we are alcoholics and addicts and our disease is very patient—it waits for that moment to grab us when we least expect it. We know from our active using and drinking days how insidious, cunning, baffling, and powerful the disease can be, and the disease doesn't lose all its power just because we become sober. Relapse can take us quickly back to that dark pit. We may think, "Just one more drink, one more hit and I'll quit tomorrow." Yet the drinks keep coming, the drugs don't stop, and tomorrow turns into years.

We're all familiar with the gut-wrenching feeling of waking up wondering, "How did this happen again?" As mothers, we owe it to our children to do whatever it takes to stay sober. We brought these children into the world, and it's our job to take care of them. If we don't take care of our disease, there's no way we can take care of our children. Think of being on a plane in an emergency, when the oxygen masks drop down in front of you. Not doing the work it takes to stay in recovery is like choosing to not put on your mask *or* your children's masks. Or your house is on fire and you choose to sit inside the burning house and do nothing. Meanwhile your children watch you lie on the couch while the flames burn around all of you and the smoke overcomes you. What makes it even sadder for you and your children is that the disease of addiction is treatable. And knowing our triggers and danger points may help us prevent a relapse, stop the family legacy of addiction, and be an example of recovery.

I went to AA to get sober because I thought I would lose my children, but I eventually decided to stay for me. Often I didn't want to go to an AA meeting because my disease told me *Those people are weird* or *I'm too busy* or *I want to drink like normal drinkers.* And often it said *Go ahead, you can have just one drink.* But when I did go to a meeting, I would hear just what I needed to hear. Once a woman shared how she had been sober for many years and then stopped going to meetings for all the reasons I mentioned above. Soon after, she took a drink and eventually she lost custody of her children. Hearing this was like having someone throw a bucket of ice water over my head—it woke me up and reminded me just how powerful this disease really is.

Triggers come in all forms, and many do involve people, places, and things. Examples of situational triggers can be places or events you associate with drinking. My friend Laura asked, "How will I ever eat Mexican food without a margarita? *Ay, caramba!* What a tragedy!" However, in recovery Laura was taught to "think through a drink": hit replay on your last drink. She remembered her last drunk and where that got her. She was dirty, disgusted, and demoralized. She knew that even one little sip of a margarita could take her back there. Now she orders a diet cola with lime when she eats tacos or burritos. When she's out with friends, she has more fun—and she remembers it the next day!

We may be avid baseball fans and think, *No way can I go to the ballpark without drinking beer.* Again, when we see this as a trigger we can slow down, make a plan, and discuss it with another alcoholic. We may or may not decide that we're ready to take in a game. In early sobriety, we might not yet realize how the disease works fully enough to understand that these situations might threaten our recovery. No matter how long anyone is sober, addicts who think *Oh, I've got this thing licked* can find themselves in danger when the addiction sneaks up behind them and says, *Go ahead, you can have just one drink or hit.*

Other triggers are family and friends. Perhaps we always drank to handle the weird feelings that came up at family gatherings. Remember the saying "Our parents can push our buttons because they installed them." Today we can avoid this trigger to use by either not going to family events or taking a sober friend with us. Bookending also helps. This means we make a commitment to call a sober friend on the way there and as soon as we leave. In our drinking and using days, we might have been the first to get to the party and the last to leave. In sobriety, we can do just the opposite: be the last to arrive and the first to leave.

Perhaps you have a certain group of girlfriends who don't get together without multiple bottles of wine in tow. Attending such a gathering can be a trigger, because we might want to fit in and not appear different. It can be difficult to let go of your old life and not feel a part of the group. Old friends might not be ready for the new sober you and may not understand why you can't have just one. Deciding not to go today doesn't mean you're never going to spend time with these friends again; it just means that you prefer to have a firm foundation in your new sober life before you put yourself in that situation.

Another benefit of Twelve Step recovery is that you'll be surrounded by rooms full of women who are living the sober life. These women will become your friends and you'll find sober people enjoying all types of activities. There are informal groups who play baseball, go bowling, meet for coffee, hike, go to women's retreats together, and so on. Attending recovery conventions and conferences are another great way to spend time with your new sober sisters.

At recovery meetings, we hear all the time about people who have relapsed on pain medication. Some doctors seem to hand these out like candy, and believe it or not, many don't understand addiction. Most doctors only have a few hours of addiction training in medical school. Pain medication drugs are so highly addictive that there is now an epidemic of their overuse. When a sober addict takes pain medication, addiction can soon rear its ugly head yet again.

Mary had been sober for more than twenty years and was very active in AA. Then she had surgery and was prescribed painkillers after the operation. Mary thought, *Oh, I never had a problem with drugs, I'm just an alcoholic,* so she left the hospital with what seemed like a truckload of medications. Though she started with the best of intentions, she was soon playing doctor, taking the medication more frequently than prescribed. Shortly after, she found herself obsessing about running out of pills and wondering how to get more. And she certainly didn't want anyone to know about any of this!

Thank God Mary was involved in AA, because while she was sitting in a women's meeting one day, she realized she was in trouble. She raised her hand and introduced herself as a newcomer. Mary feels so fortunate that she was able to get back to recovery after this relapse. Talk to your doctor about whether it is truly necessary for you to have pain medication; if it is, find someone you trust to administer the medication. And be sure to discuss this issue with your sponsor so you can be accountable to her as well.

Other contributing factors for relapse, which few doctors and experts in the addiction field address, are PMS, menopause, and hormonal shifts. I'm no doctor, but this matches my personal experience and that of many other women I know. I had no idea my hormones were out of whack, and I felt like my extreme moods were pushing me toward a mental and emotional breakdown. Although I didn't relapse on drugs and alcohol, I felt like I wanted to crawl out of my skin and punch the hell out of an innocent bystander.

I thought doing a Fourth Step inventory would help get rid of what felt like anger. I went to more meetings, thinking that would do it. I tried to get out of myself and help more women, yet none of this was working. My symptoms were many: my mood went from high to low, my thinking grew foggy, my legs were cramping, I had horrible headaches, I wasn't sleeping well at night, and my stomach was so bloated it looked like I was pregnant. I finally started looking for help when my feelings of depression intensified and I had crying bouts that lasted all day long. I went to my general practitioner but all she did was draw blood to test my thyroid. It was fine, and she concluded I was perfectly healthy. Then I went to my gynecologist and she handed me a pamphlet on menopause and told me to read it. She said my symptoms didn't sound too bad, so she suggested I do nothing. Again, I am not a doctor, and our bodies are all different. I can't recommend a particular course of action. But I can report that I finally found help from a female psychiatrist who understood addiction and how hormones affect recovery and cravings.

Helen, a sober friend of mine, has had multiple relapses. She was a prescription drug abuser and, time after time, she relapsed after thirty days of sobriety. Over a six-year period, she went to three treatment centers and sought out doctor after doctor trying to get help. She lost her job due to emotional outbursts; her kids said they felt like they were walking on eggshells when she was around. Her husband said he was on the verge of filing for a divorce because the sweet woman he married had been kidnapped and replaced with a psychotic crazy woman. He had no idea what was going on with her as he suffered the brunt of her yelling and frustration. They had tried marriage counseling for more than a year but nothing seemed to improve. Finally, when she found help for her hormonal imbalance, she got clean from the pills. Her husband said he felt like he got his real wife back.

Certain feelings can lead us to relapse if we're not paying attention. Fear, resentment, hopelessness, and despair can creep up on us at any moment. At these times, it's very important to stay close to our sponsor, attend meetings, and talk about our feelings. The worst thing you can do is to isolate and stuff your feelings. Begin to become aware of your own triggers, make a list of things that can set you off, and make a plan for responding to the Danger sign: slow down and take action to go in a healthy direction.

Sober Mom's Tools
for Avoiding Relapse and Recognizing Triggers

1. List your triggers: people, places, and things to avoid. Then create an action plan for what you will do when confronted with one of these situations.

2. Make a list of activities you could do immediately when you have a craving. For example, go for a walk, call a sober friend, go to a meeting.

3. Carry a list of Twelve Step people you can call. When you have the craving, call and talk to someone about it immediately.

4. Learn coping skills like relaxation exercises and meditation to manage stress.

• • •

24

Life Vision

There are only seven days in the week and
"someday" is not one of them.

— RITA CHAND

The beauty about being a life coach and an AA sponsor is that I get to see women go from self-hatred to loving and honoring themselves. I truly believe that in Twelve Step programs we uncover and discover who we really are underneath all the shame.

When I was eleven years sober, I spent some time reflecting on the past decade of my life in recovery. During those years, I had done many Twelve Step programs, gone through a lot of therapy and spent much time soul-searching. I asked myself, *Where do I see myself in five years? What do I want to be doing? What gifts do I want to offer the world? What would I like to create?* I really had no idea how to answer these questions at first, but I had overcome so many challenges by working through the Twelve Steps that I thought maybe they could help me here as well. I decided to apply the Twelve Steps with a different twist. Here's how I adapted the Steps to help me develop a vision for my life and then take the action necessary to achieve that vision.

Step 1. I have power over my thoughts, attitudes, responses, actions, reactions, and choices, and these can always be positive and beneficial to others and myself. I am 100 percent responsible for my life today. *Action Step:* Write a Life Vision statement. How exactly would you like your life to be, financially, spiritually, emotionally, socially, physically, and mentally? Write it in the present tense, as if it is already true. For example: I am fit and trim, and I run five miles four times a week. I make $_____, spend one third, save one third, and give one third away. I own successful companies that are world-renowned and help others change their lives.

Step 2. I believe a Higher Power is a source of powerful positive thoughts and ideas. This source lives within others and me. *Action Step:* Whenever you think a negative thought or hear one from someone else, change the statement to one that is positive and in the present tense. For example, if that voice in your head says "I feel fat," change it to "I'm so glad I am fit and toned. I thank God for all the wonderful food I have been given." If you hear "I don't have enough money," change it to "I have plenty of money, and abundant resources are all around me!" Also ask yourself, "What one thing am I not doing that could help change this situation?" For example, to change my "I'm fat" feeling, I decided to exercise for an hour every day. To turn around the "I don't have enough money" story, I decided to find a job. So when everybody else started work at eight a.m., I did likewise: I sat down at my computer and worked until five p.m. on finding a job.

Step 3. Every day I design and co-create my life with the help of a Higher Power of my choice. *Action Step:* In the morning write a description of exactly how you'd like your day to go. Keep in mind your vision statement. Close your eyes and envision this: *God is right next to me throughout my day.*

Step 4. I write a list of all the good qualities and talents I have been given, and the talents and abilities I'd like to develop. *Action Step:* Review this list every morning and set an intention to use at least one of the qualities you already have that day. Then choose one of the skills or abilities you'd like to develop and make a commitment to do one thing today towards achieving that goal.

Step 5. I share my list of talents and desired qualities with a supportive mentor who holds me accountable to myself and the commitments I made in step four. *Action Step:* Ask five people to name a quality or talent they see in you (you may ask more than five). Add these to your list. Read over your list first thing in the morning and last thing at night.

Step 6. I connect to the Higher Power within me to help me use these talents and abilities to improve my life and the lives of those around me, especially my children's. *Action Step:* List one thing you can do today toward achieving your Life Vision and then do it. (You can do more than one. Remember, this is your life!) Try to do one in each category. Stretch yourself and do something each day that scares you!

Step 7. I humbly ask my Higher Power to fill me with a creative idea or action and empower me to carry it out. *Action Step:* Sit down with paper and pen and think about your Life Vision statement. Write down every idea that comes to you to help you move closer to these goals, even if they seem crazy. I often say to my Higher Power, "Are you crazy?"

Step 8. I make a list of all the good I have done in my life and I see what has made me feel really happy about myself. *Action Step:* At the end of each day, jot down in your journal a few things you did well. For example, "I exercised, I ate a healthy breakfast, and I told my son I loved him." Include on this list the things you take for granted that you do regularly, such as "I go to work, I take the kids to school, I smile at strangers."

Step 9. I make a list of all the good I would like to bring to my children, the rest of my family, friends, coworkers, the community, the world, and myself. *Action Step:* Do one thing each day for someone else or for the planet, and don't let anyone know.

Step 10. I take time to think about all the things I am grateful for. *Action Step:* Write a daily gratitude list. Remember to include things you have in your vision statement; for example, "I'm so grateful that the perfect job I'm looking for is coming to me."

Step 11. I pray and meditate daily on my Life Vision. I connect to the Higher Power within me for the power and guidance to achieve that vision. *Action Step:* Read your vision statement twice daily—first thing in the morning and before you fall asleep at night. Close your eyes for a minimum of five minutes and envision yourself exactly as you described in your Life Vision. Feel the emotions that come up for you as go through this process.

Step 12. I repeat these steps daily. *Action Step:* Watch your life change right before your very own eyes! Share this experience with another person. Share your experience with another woman in recovery and support her on her journey. Include your children in your journey.

I create a "vision board" every January where I picture what I want to have happen in my life in the new year. I have also facilitated workshops and worked with my clients individually to help them gain clarity on their visions for their own lives, create an action plan, and take steps toward creating what they want in life. Some yearn for a partner, a better relationship with their children, a home, more travel, or more money. Others want to find a passion, sell their art, expand their business, deepen their spiritual life, change careers, or reduce stress in their life. What I find most interesting is that whenever I suggest adding their Higher Power to the process, miracles start happening. Doors seem to open up, an opportunity presents itself out of nowhere, a person appears just at the right time, or another sudden co-incidence occurs. I am not sure how or why it works; I just know the results I've seen and the reports I've heard from my clients and sponsees as they share their progress.

Sober Mom's Tools
for Creating Your Life Vision

1. Work through the Twelve Step exercise above.

2. Create a vision board. Draw or cut out pictures from maga-zines that represent your dreams, hopes, and goals. Paste them onto poster board and hang the board where you can see it daily.

3. Talk to your children about how your life vision includes them and their welfare.

4. Take one step and meditate on it for a week. Try to medi-tate for at least five minutes every day. After each meditation, journal about what came up in your meditation. If nothing does, it's perfectly fine. Give yourself a hand for sitting still and focusing on that aspect of your life vision. Sometime just sitting quietly and clearing the brain is good. Repeat in the same manner each week until you have meditated on the other eleven steps.

• • •

25

Ho, Ho, Ho, and the Not-So-Merry Holidays

Good news: The holidays are about family.
Bad news: It's your own family.

— BUMPER STICKER

Bells are ringing, chestnuts are roasting, Santa's on his way, and you smile to all passersby, saying "Happy holidays!" when really you want to vomit up fruitcake.

The holidays can be so stressful. The shopping, traffic, lines at the stores, events at work and school can turn the Hallmark holiday into Hallmark hell. Money can be tight, and your kids want the newest gizmo that costs three times your gift budget. And to top it off, there is alcohol everywhere you look.

When we were drinking or using we could be counted on to throw a wrench into a holiday gathering—yep, we were capable of being the Grinch. A Tim Whyatt cartoon says, "Every family has one weird relative, and if you don't know who it is, then it's probably you." Having an active addict in the family is like having a ticking time bomb; you know it's going to go off but you don't know when.

In recovery, we can laugh about the holidays and some of our antics from our drinking or using days. Holiday parties are often a source of lots of laughs. Alcoholic or drugs + party = disaster! So many of us have been completely inappropriate and humiliated ourselves while drunk or high at the office or neighborhood party. I remember one AA member's story about her company's evening holiday party. Drunk by ten-thirty, she told her boss "how she honestly felt about him." By midnight she was making out with a married man in a coat closet. It was a three-ring circus. Needless to say, the mood in her office on Monday morning was frosty.

Yep, while drinking or using we were evil little elves. It was a cinch for us to do absolutely the wrong thing, with the wrong people, at the wrong time—and we may have even lost our clothes, our jobs, or our neighborhood friends in the process.

Most of us have such huge expectations about how the holidays should be for our families and our children. We want everything to be perfect! We picture our loving family gathered around the holiday dinner table, smiling and laughing. In the past, our holidays may have been anything but lovely affairs. One woman described what happened in her home one holiday. Her uncle set fire to the Christmas tree, her dad was so drunk he carved and served a half-cooked turkey, and her cousin once again ended up inebriated and crying in the corner of the living room.

I got sober November 13, 1999. I was separated from my then husband. Our children were two, five, and eight years old. Within the next six weeks, I had to face Thanksgiving, my daughter's birthday, my son's birthday, Christmas Eve, Christmas Day, and the new millennium! I prayed that the holidays would just be over with. *How the hell am I not going to drink through all of this?* I wondered. In the end, I did stay sober through this first holiday season by taking it one day at a time, just like every other day I was sober. Actually most days were one hour at a time. I also went to a lot of AA meetings and listened to people share their fears about being with family, going to parties where alcohol was being served, and surviving the loneliness and stress of the holidays.

The most difficult holiday for me that year was Christmas. It had always been my favorite holiday. But this year, I had been sober for only forty-three days. Although we were separated, my husband and I had planned to spend Christmas morning together at my house with the children. It wasn't the cheerful Christmas morning I was used to, with the kids jumping on my husband and me in bed, waking us to tell us Santa had brought them lots of presents. Instead, my kids came running into my bedroom to see me sleeping alone. I had to call their daddy to let him know the kids were up and he could hurry on over. I tried to keep our kids patient and wait to open presents until their dad showed up. My eight-year-old said, "This sucks. Why didn't daddy just stay here last night?" All I could say was, "Hang on, he'll be here in a minute." I tried to hide my wrenching pain—the guilt and anger I felt that my kids had also been affected by my drinking. I did what my sponsor had suggested and just tried to focus on my kids.

After the gifts were opened, we headed for the airport. My husband was going to drop the kids and me off so we could fly out to visit my parents. Then, all of a sudden I was overcome with sadness that we were no longer a unified family. I broke down and begged my husband to take me back and reunite the family. What I really wanted was a fantasy, the fantasy of the picture-perfect family on Christmas. All three kids and I were crying. My soon-to-be-ex was wise enough to know what I craved was an illusion. He said to me, "It's the emotion-charged holidays talking. Go to your parents' and have a good time." When we arrived at my parents all I could do was run into the bathroom and cry, dry my eyes, and once again try to focus on my kids and family. All I wanted was for the day to end.

In recovery, I learned invaluable tools to get me through such challenging times, experiences I didn't even know I would be facing. In the rooms of AA, I heard suggestions on what to do and what not to do to survive the holidays. And when the time came to use those suggestions, I thought those people in AA were brilliant.

Here are some tips I've found most helpful for surviving holiday gatherings without drinking, using, or going loco.

Most important, say to yourself, *My sobriety comes first,* even before Santa Claus, relatives, or my job. We think we are obligated to go wherever we are invited, but in recovery we learn that we need to take care of ourselves first and foremost. So don't go to all the parties where alcohol will be served or people will be high! The party will go on without you. Don't put your recovery in jeopardy by going to a "slippery place." If you really must go a holiday event, take a sober friend with you. And plan your transportation so you can leave if you feel shaky; then immediately call your sponsor or go to a meeting. It helps to be with our sober tribe when we are feeling vulnerable. At parties, always have a glass of juice or soda in your hand, so people won't be offering you drinks. If someone insists you have an alcoholic beverage, tell them you are the designated driver, or that you're allergic to alcohol, or if you're comfortable revealing it to this person, just say that you are in recovery. It often helps to keep busy; the hostess will love you if you help serve or clean. If at any time you feel like you are going to drink, leave the party ASAP.

What *not* to do at the holiday gatherings: Do not try to Twelve Step anyone who may be enjoying a glass or two. When someone asks if you would like a drink, don't feel you have to tell them you are an alcoholic and recite your entire "drunka-log." It's none of their business, unless it happens to be someone you trust and feel comfortable revealing this with. Remember: boundaries! Keep your sense of humor; thank God that today you won't be sleeping with your boss's husband and get run out of town!

Of course, as mothers in recovery we want to make the dream holiday for our family. We may even try to make up for all the holidays that were not so good. But these efforts can get us into trouble. With the help of our sponsors and friends, we can learn how to take it easy, not put so much stress on ourselves, and still enjoy our holidays while sober.

When I was drinking, I'd throw extravagant parties, spending money we didn't have, making sure the house looked like a showplace from *Better Homes and Gardens* magazine, the entire family outfitted in picture-perfect clothes. Of course I also had to make sure we had plenty of alcohol in stock. By the end of the night, I was always a screaming mess. And the next day, the house was in shambles and so was I.

In sobriety, I have created new traditions. When the children were small, we'd decorate a gingerbread house together. I'd invite my best friend to come over with her two boys, and we'd play games, charades, Jesters, and Pictionary. Everyone laughed all night and we all looked forward to the gathering all year. One year the kids and I bought a bunch of hats and scarves and handed them out to homeless people; besides helping others, the kids got to see how good they have it. Enjoying the holidays with your children (and enjoying the child in yourself) is probably the best way to get a safe holiday high.

I have also learned that I don't have to overspend during the holidays and send the family budget into a free fall. Some of the best gifts are inexpensive funny or meaningful items. I know a woman who wanted to give a special gift to her friend but she was broke; she found bubble bath in a bottle shaped like a pink poodle. It was silly but heartfelt. The woman she gave it to kept it for years and said it was the best gift she received that holiday.

A coaching client of mine, Emily, was dreading the holidays. She had lost custody of her children and thought she would never survive her first holiday sober. The pain, shame, and loneliness she felt were almost overwhelming. She shared these feelings at her women's meeting, and afterward other women came up to her and embraced her with love and hope. She met other women who were in similar situations and they decided to stick together during this hard time. They checked in on each other and went to the local AA marathon meetings called Alcathons, held in some cities. These twenty-four-hour events have saved many an addict during the holidays. Typically an Alcathon starts at noon on the day before the holiday: Thanksgiving, Christmas Day, and New Year's Day. Meetings often start every hour continuously until the next day at noon. Emily said being with people in recovery saved her at these times, and she made herself useful by making coffee and taking care of the refreshment table.

When I was working at a recovery center, a woman called right before the holidays and asked to make a reservation for her husband to come in for treatment on January 2. She said they had too many family dinners and celebrations planned for him to stop drinking before then. I asked, "Ma'am, how was your holiday last year?" She gasped and said, "Oh, I see; he'd better come in right now."

We all tend to romanticize the past and forget just how bad it was. This holiday season, give yourself and your children the best present you'll ever get—the grace of being sober.

Sober Mom's Tools
for Surviving the Holidays

1. Put your sobriety first. Do what you need to do to stay sane and sober. Call other sober women and go to lots of meetings. Don't put unreasonable expectations on yourself. Your children will enjoy any holiday when their mom is sober and focused on them.

2. Practice an attitude of gratitude. Be thankful for the small things: that you woke up sober, that you have another day to experience the grace of being a new you. Today you are part of the solution instead of part of the problem.

3. Practice a spirit of giving. Do a good deed without getting found out: perhaps leave a present for an elderly neighbor, adopt a family, or simply make cookies and take them to your favorite AA meeting.

4. Remember, it's just another day. Root for midnight, go to bed, and tell yourself you can drink tomorrow. My experience tells me you will wake up grateful you did not drink yesterday.

• • •

26

Forgiveness of Others and Self

*Life becomes easier when you learn to accept
the apology you never got.*

— ROBERT BRAULT

Forgiveness does not *excuse* the behavior of someone who may have harmed or hurt you. The offending person might be quite wrong and may have done real harm. When we forgive, we do not have to invite this person into our lives. We don't have to spend time with him or her or pretend we are okay with what happened in the past. Forgiving is really about our own well-being and peace of mind. Forgiveness means you have decided to free the other person and yourself from the prison of resentment. I once heard someone say, "When you choose to forgive those who have hurt you, you take their power away." In making the decision to forgive, we are throwing away the keys to the ball and chain that we have been dragging around behind us.

A client of mine named Jennifer described a time when she grew from anger to forgiveness. She had a huge fight with her husband on the phone, and she was really upset with him. After she slammed the phone down, she went to pick up her crying baby out of his crib. When she did, she noticed his tiny little hands were just like her husband's. All of a sudden her heart softened. At that moment, Jennifer was grateful for her husband, because without him she wouldn't have her beautiful son and his tiny precious hands. As she reached out and held her son's hand, the angry feelings melted away. The disagreement she'd been so upset about five minutes ago didn't seem like a big deal anymore, and she forgave both her husband and herself. Sometimes all it takes is a conscious decision to soften our heart, and we begin to forgive.

When I had been divorced for nine years and sober for ten, life gave me a lesson about forgiving and letting go. I had done many Fourth Steps, lots of self-reflection, and I'd made a lot of amends to myself and others. But still, my hard feelings and old moldy resentment around my ex-husband would creep up on me. One day, I was out of town at my son's basketball tournament when I got a call from my ex-husband telling me he had cancer. Oh God, I thought, it was the news no one wants to hear. When I hung up the phone, I burst into tears. Suddenly a flood of warmth, love, and compassion washed out any hint of the anger I was still holding toward this man. It's a shame that it takes such tragedy for us to wake up and let go of our old feelings of resentment. Now I was in fear that he would die and my children would be without a father. Feelings of regret for all the harm I had done to him over the years flooded me like a storm. Feeling overwhelmed, I immediately did what I was taught to do when a storm strikes in my life: I called my best friend Lori and bawled my eyes out. I was in complete panic for my ex-husband and for my kids. Lori reminded me he was still alive, I was okay in this moment, and I needed to return to the present and focus on my son's basketball game.

What I love about my friends in Twelve Step programs is they remind me which program tools I need to pick up when I have lost my way. And as I often say, "Thank God we aren't all crazy at the same time. We get to take turns!"

That day Lori helped me pick up the tool of staying in the moment, being present for my child, and trusting in the unknown. AA taught me to get out of myself when I am struggling and to be of service. Instead of focusing on my fear when I got back from the trip, I brought dinner to my ex's new family and asked what I could do to help. In the days and months to come, I watched my ex-husband walk through his cancer with strength, courage, and a lot of humor. After all his hair fell out, he bought a convertible and told everyone he'd always wanted one but was afraid his hair would get messed up. He said with a laugh, "Now I don't have to worry about my hair anymore!" After he got his health back he joined a cycling team to raise money for the Lymphoma Leukemia Society. His cancer is in remission and he continues to ride in the annual charity event, raising large sums of money for the cause.

I realized that through his disease, my ex-husband was teaching our children how to face fears, show up one day at a time, and help another who is still suffering. Ironically, my disease taught our children the same. He was treating his disease of cancer by showing up for chemotherapy and radiation. I was treating my disease of alcoholism by showing up at AA. I had a lot of compassion for him and his disease but I still found that I was beating myself up for the damage my disease caused my family. I finally saw my life in perspective and understood that our broken places are actually gifts and our family grew closer because of them. This realization helped me let go and forgive him, and now it was time to really let go and forgive myself.

We can be prompted to forgive in the strangest ways. One of the highlights of my recovery was reading my daughter's school paper about a person she admired. While most students wrote about some truly heroic person, she chose to write about me because she had seen all the trials I had overcome. Her paper helped me put down the stick I'd been beating myself with for so many years, thinking I'd permanently damaged my children. When one of our sons was assigned a similar project, he wrote about his father. In his paper, he explained that he chose his father because he was so brave for enduring his cancer treatments—and for going out in public with no hair! Letting go of old anger and resentment allowed me to be present for all of this. Forgiveness doesn't happen all at once. It is a process, and by working through this process I experienced the power of healing and restoring a bond that had been broken and that now enriches my life.

Holding on to resentments can cause a deadly corrosion of self. In Step Eight we make a list of all persons we have harmed. How many of us forget to put ourselves on the list? We harmed ourselves while we were drinking or using. Our thoughts and actions caused pain to ourselves, not just to others. We are our own worst critics. Self-forgiveness is something we can practice daily. As women, we often tend to hold on to the harms we have done, and perhaps we even think we don't deserve to be forgiven. Self-loathing can lead to relapse, so it is essential we learn to soften our hearts towards ourselves.

The most painful stories I've heard in the rooms of AA have been from the mothers who have lost their children due to their addictions. A mother's primary instinct is to take care of her children, nurture them, provide for them, and protect them. And yet the grip of our addiction is so strong it can cause us to abandon and neglect our most precious gift—our children. The average person would never understand how a mother could neglect or even endanger her own child, but we who have been there know the disease can become even more powerful than the maternal instinct at times.

One woman recalled that while she was pregnant, she knew that she wouldn't be able to take care of the baby—she couldn't even take care of herself. One day when the little boy was only months old, she told the father she was going to the Laundromat—and she never came back. She went back to the streets. It took her years to finally get sober: anytime her mind started to clear after a few days of sobriety, the shame of walking out on her son was so unbearable that she'd pick up another bottle. She was one of the lucky ones, though. She finally got sober and eventually got her son back.

So many women come into recovery having lost custody of their children—to the children's father, to another family member, or to foster care. Children sometimes want nothing to do with their mother because she embarrassed or neglected them. The children can become angry and hurt and often these feelings do not go away overnight, if ever.

A screaming or passed-out mother is not the ideal picture of motherhood. We can't expect our family to welcome us with open arms just because we get sober; it takes lots of time and patience to regain that trust and respect. Our parents, significant others, and children may think, *So what? She's sober now, but she shouldn't have caused us this worry and pain in the first place.*

Many women never regain their families but, through working the Twelve Steps, they are still able to forgive themselves and move forward in their lives. Karen shared her story. She was a suburban housewife married for fifteen years with a thirteen-year-old son and a seven-year-old daughter. Her drinking and drugging got so bad that her husband divorced her and filed for sole custody, which he easily won. Karen says, "I had failed as a mother, failed as a wife. My purpose was to be a mother, and without my kids I had no identity."

After the children were gone and she was alone, she used even more. She graduated to hard drugs, anything to mask the pain of losing her children. Karen's life spiraled out of control; she was arrested for possession and went to jail many times. She met a man who used and drank too, and they had a daughter named Hannah. Neither of them was fit to take care of Hannah. One night her boyfriend beat Karen up, held a gun to her temple and cocked it. Karen was holding seven-month-old Hannah at the time. Karen said, "Do you want your daughter's last memory of her mother to be her blood splattered on the wall?" He walked into another room, and Karen called 911. The SWAT team came and there was a six-hour standoff.

The police arrested both Karen and Hannah's dad. She remembers the policewoman looking at her with disgust. It's the look many of us saw in the eyes of people when we were using, part pity and part incomprehensible revulsion, the look that says, *How could you do this?* The officer called Child Protective Services to take Hannah to emergency foster care. As Karen was sobbing and begging the officer not to take her daughter, she asked to kiss her before she was taken. The officer said, "No. Your daughter needs more than food and diapers, your little girl needs care, protection, and love." Karen was furious and heartbroken as the van drove away with her child.

The officers arrested Karen then and there for numerous outstanding warrants. She was sentenced to three months in jail. In her cell, she had nothing to do but think about what a disaster her life had become and her own inability to take care of her own child. She worried about Hannah all the time. It drove her crazy to not know what kind of family her daughter was with or if anyone was comforting her.

After Karen was released, she was sent to a six-month treatment program. While she was in this facility, the court allowed Karen to have short supervised visits with Hannah. After treatment, Karen finally got an apartment, and two years after Hannah was taken away, the court let her come live with her mother. Today Karen has five continuous years of sobriety and many of us have seen Hannah grow up in the rooms of AA.

Even though Karen has made amends to her older children, they still want nothing to do with her and won't respond to her letters and calls. But the truth is that we can stay sober and clean no matter what befalls us. We can even learn to live with heartbreaking disappointments and *not* drink or use. Karen has worked to heal and forgive herself. She said that what helped her heal the most was listening to stories of other women who lost their own children. She did not feel judged by these women. They were compassionate and loving toward her, and they showed her how to treat herself the same way. Karen's healing continues as she reaches out to other women who have lost their children due to their addictions. In recovery our stories become our greatest gifts.

We enter the path to happiness when we learn to forgive ourselves and others. One of the greatest gifts we can give our children is showing them by example that forgiveness of self and others is the path to happiness. When our children see us treating ourselves with compassion they learn to treat themselves the same way.

Sober Mom's Tools
for Forgiving Yourself and Others

1. Learn to be gentle with yourself. If your child made a mistake, what would you say? Rather than shaming your child, you'd likely listen and offer encouragement, saying that everyone makes mistakes: that's why pencils have erasers and computer keyboards have "delete" keys!

2. Write yourself an "I forgive you" letter as if you were writing it to your best friend.

3. Make a Letting Go Box—Get a box or bag and decorate it with paint and stickers if you like. Then, on slips of paper, write the names of all the people you are having a hard time forgiving—and don't forget to put yourself on the list. Next, place the slips in the box and let them go.

4. Send good intentions or prayers to someone you resent or have not forgiven. Praying for someone we resent will set us free, as the Big Book tells us (page 552):

> If you have resentment you want to be free of, if you will pray for the person or thing that you resent, you will be free. If you will ask in prayer for everything you want for yourself to be given to them, you will be free. Ask for their health, their prosperity, their happiness, and you will be free. Even when you don't really want it for them and your prayers are only words and you don't mean it, go ahead and do it anyway. Do it every day for two weeks, and you will find you have come to mean it and to want it for them, and you will realize that where you used to feel bitterness and resentment and hatred, you now feel compassionate understanding and love.

• • •

The Twelve Steps of Alcoholics Anonymous

1. We admitted we were powerless over alcohol—that our lives had become unmanageable.
2. Came to believe that a Power greater than ourselves could restore us to sanity.
3. Made a decision to turn our will and our lives over to the care of God *as we understood Him.*
4. Made a searching and fearless moral inventory of ourselves.
5. Admitted to God, to ourselves, and to another human being the exact nature of our wrongs.
6. Were entirely ready to have God remove all these defects of character.
7. Humbly asked Him to remove our shortcomings.
8. Made a list of all persons we had harmed, and became willing to make amends to them all.
9. Made direct amends to such people wherever possible, except when to do so would injure them or others.
10. Continued to take personal inventory and when we were wrong promptly admitted it.
11. Sought through prayer and meditation to improve our conscious contact with God *as we understood Him,* praying only for knowledge of His will for us and the power to carry that out.
12. Having had a spiritual awakening as the result of these steps, we tried to carry this message to alcoholics, and to practice these principles in all our affairs.

The Twelve Steps of Alcoholics Anonymous are taken from *Alcoholics Anonymous,* 4th ed. (New York: Alcoholics Anonymous World Services, 2001), 59–60.

Recommended Resources

Recovery Organizations

Alcoholics Anonymous: www.aa.org

Al-Anon Family Groups: www.al-anon.alateen.org

Co-Dependents Anonymous: www.coda.org

Love Addicts Anonymous: www.loveaddicts.org

Narcotics Anonymous: www.na.org

Nar-Anon Family Groups: www.naranon.org

Sex and Love Addicts Anonymous: www.slaafws.org

Books

Alcoholics Anonymous, 4th edition (New York: Alcoholics Anonymous World Services, Inc., 2001).

Each Day a New Beginning: Daily Meditations for Women by Karen Casey (Center City, MN: Hazelden, 1991).

Narcotics Anonymous, 6th edition (Van Nuys, CA: Narcotics Anonymous World Services, Inc., 2008).

Paths to Recovery: Al-Anon's Steps, Traditions, and Concepts (New York: Al-Anon Family Groups Headquarters, Inc., 1997).

The Recovering Heart: Emotional Sobriety for Women by Beverly Conyers (Center City, MN: Hazelden, 2013).

Twelve Steps and Twelve Traditions (New York: Alcoholics Anonymous World Services, Inc., 2012).

A Woman's Way through the Twelve Steps by Stephanie Covington (Center City, MN: Hazelden, 1994).

About the Author

Rosemary O'Connor is a certified addiction recovery coach and certified professional coach. She founded ROC Recovery Services (rocrecoveryservices.com) to respond to the specific needs of women and mothers in recovery. ROC offers supportive recovery homes, recovery coaching, life coaching, sober companions, and experiential workshops to support and teach simple solutions for continued long-term recovery. Rosemary's mission is to help women recover from the devastating effects of addiction, and to teach them how to live a rewarding life of purpose and meaningful connection to self and others.

In 1999, as the mother of three small children, Rosemary made the most important decision of her life: she entered into recovery from her alcoholism. A graduate of St. Mary's College of California, Rosemary lives in Northern California. She insists on having fun and loves to hike and swim in the San Francisco Bay.

About Hazelden Publishing

As part of the Hazelden Betty Ford Foundation, Hazelden Publishing offers both cutting-edge educational resources and inspirational books. Our print and digital works help guide individuals in treatment and recovery, and their loved ones. Professionals who work to prevent and treat addiction also turn to Hazelden Publishing for evidence-based curricula, digital content solutions, and videos for use in schools, treatment programs, correctional programs, and electronic health records systems. We also offer training for implementation of our curricula.

Through published and digital works, Hazelden Publishing extends the reach of healing and hope to individuals, families, and communities affected by addiction and related issues.

For more information about Hazelden publications,
please call **800-328-9000**
or visit us online at **hazelden.org/bookstore**.

Also of Interest

A Woman's Way through the Twelve Steps
Stephanie S. Covington, PhD
Acknowledging that recovery raises special issues for women—from questions about sexuality, relationships, and everyday life to anxieties about speaking up at mixed-gender meetings—this book focuses directly on women's experience of addiction and healing. The Twelve Steps are illuminated to empower the reader to take ownership of her own recovery.
Order No. 5019; ebook EB5019; in Spanish 2659

The Recovering Heart: Emotional Sobriety for Women
Beverly Conyers
Your old, destructive lifestyle is fading into the past. What an amazing gift you've given yourself with your recovery. So why aren't you happier? As sobriety takes hold and your head starts to clear, a wide range of emotions can begin to emerge. To stay sober, and to grow and flourish, you must engage in healing and take responsibility for these long-neglected emotions.
Order No. 3969; ebook EB3969

Each Day a New Beginning: Daily Meditations for Women
Karen Casey
Each day holds its promise, and life's journey begins anew. Let this book be your companion, lightening your burdens and heightening your joys with its daily offering of the gentle warmth and wise counsel of women traveling the same road.
Order No. 1076; ebook EB1076; in Spanish 4387.

Also available: iPhone app (AP1076) from the iTunes/Apple App Store; Android app (AA1076) from the Google/Android App store.

These Hazelden titles are available through
bookstores everywhere and online at
hazelden.org/bookstore.